Karen Rockenbach

The Craft of Silk and Gold Thread Embroidery and Stump Work

ERICA WILSON

CHARLES SCRIBNER'S SONS / NEW YORK

Library of Congress Cataloging in Publication Data

Wilson, Erica.
The craft of silk and gold thread embroidery, and stump work.

"Taken from two sections in Erica Wilson's embroidery book."
1. Embroidery. 2. Gold thread. 3. Silk thread.
I. Title.
TT770.W538 746.4'4 77-23349
ISBN 0-684-15067-0

1 3 5 7 9 11 13 15 17 19 Q/P 20 18 16 14 12 10 8 6 4 2

PRINTED IN THE UNITED STATES OF AMERICA

SILK AND GOLD THREADS

. . . Allso the Vice-chancellour presented a paire of gloves, perfumed and garnished with embroiderie and goldsmiths worke, price 60s. . . . In taking the book and the gloves, it fortuned that the paper in which the gloves were folded to open; and her Majestie behoulding the beautie of the said gloves, as in great admiration, and in token of hir thankful acceptation of the same, held up one of her hands; and then, smelling unto them, put them halfwaie upon hir hands. And when the oracion was ended, she rendyred and gave most heartie thanks, promising to be mindful of the Universitie.

—QUEEN ELIZABETH'S RECEPTION OF A DELEGATION FROM THE UNIVERSITY OF CAMBRIDGE, AT AUDLEY END, ESSEX, 1578

Japanese No robe, 17th century. Silk on gilded satin. *The Metropolitan Museum of Art, Pulitzer Fund, 1932*

SILK was said to have been cultivated in China by the Empress Si-Ling as early as 2640 B.C. This may be mythical but a remnant of silk still exists which dates from the fifth century B.C. Though the silkworm was held in great veneration in China (a ceremony in its honor being performed every year), silk was such a commonplace material that it was used by all classes and for almost every purpose for which fabrics might be used.

The early history of silk reads like a novel of international intrigue, for the secret of its culture was jealously guarded by the Chinese, and attempts of other countries to start their own production were constantly frustrated. However, in the fifth century A.D. the King of Kustana (Khotan) sought a marriage union with a princess of the Eastern Kingdom (China), as a token of his allegiance and submission. The Chinese Emperor agreed; whereupon the king immediately sent off messengers to the princess, saying, "Our country has neither silk nor silken stuffs. You had better bring mulberry seeds and silkworms, so that you can make robes for yourself after your arrival." So the princess smuggled both across the border, hidden in her turban, for the guards never dared to ask if they could search her there.

It is said that in the sixth century two monks traveling from Khotan brought silkworm eggs in a hollow cane to Byzantium. After the Emperor Justinian established silkworm culture at Constantinople, it was jealously guarded for nearly five hundred years. In the twelfth century Italy became a center for the manufacture of silk, and there no member of the Florentine silk guilds was allowed to leave the city without a permit, and pawnbrokers were not allowed to receive silk or any tool for its weaving.

Metallic threads, too, go back into the history of ancient lands. When you consider the importance of sun worship in early cultures, it is easy to see how gold would, in the primitive mind, seem to impart the magical properties of the sun to any article. Remains of gold and silver wire thread for embroidery have been found in a tomb in Thebes, and gold threads are often referred to in the Bible.

Embroidered glove and mitten, English 16th century. *Victoria and Albert Museum*

Part of an apparel of an alb, 14th century. Colored silks, silver and silver-gilt thread on red velvet. Background in couché rentré. *Victoria and Albert Museum*

As Moses said, "They did beat the gold into thin plates, and cut it into wires, to work in the blue and the purple, and in the scarlet and in the very fine linen." We are told that Aaron's robe, the ephod, was all blue, of one circular piece of linen with an opening for the head in the center, edged with a woven binding, and "a golden bell and a pomegranate, upon the hem of the robe round about," were wrought with "cunning work" in blue, purple, and scarlet.

Imagine the ships bearing down from Tarshish, laden with cargoes of gold, silver, ivory, apes, and peacocks, arriving at Solomon's kingdom. Since the soldiers' shields, all the drinking vessels, the ivory throne, and even the stairs of the temple, were all either made of or covered with beaten gold, we can get a glimpse of the luxury and magnificence of the costumes when we hear that the Queen of Sheba "had no more spirit in her" when she had seen, among all the other finery, the "attendance of Solomon's ministers, and their apparel, and his cupbearers and their apparel." When Solomon was building the temple, the son of a man from Tyre was brought in because he was "skillfull to work in gold, in silver and in brass, in iron, in stone and in timber, in purple, in blue and in fine linen and in crimson, also to grave any manner of graving, and to find out every device which shall be put to him, with his cunning men." He would be surely cunning indeed to be accomplished in such a wide variety of skills! But it does give us an interesting sidelight on how close the arts were to one another, for though individual craftsmen may have worked in a highly specialized manner (as later medieval craftsmen worked only within their guilds), one "overseer" would supervise a whole operation. Thus one can see how each of the arts would influence the others in design, since those who coordinated a project would have an interest and knowledge that overlapped into all media.

As the gold, beaten flat into strips, was stiff and difficult to handle, it was later found that it could be wrapped around silver bullion, which was melted down and drawn through narrower and narrower holes until, still coated with the gold, it formed a thin wire. The resulting stronger, more flexible thread was then beaten flat and twisted around a core of orange or yellow silk. This method was first developed in the Orient but a similar one is still used to this day. Gold leaf on paper is twisted around and lightly gummed to the silk, and the thread is known as "Japanese gold." Flexible, untarnishing, and of a beautiful glowing color, it can only be "couched" on the surface of the fabric, as it would naturally be spoiled by pulling it back and forth through the cloth.

The sophistication and beauty of both silk and gold thread made embroidery with these materials particularly suitable for ecclesiastical use. Only the best that the hand of man could form would be suitable for use in the house of God. One of the greatest periods in history for embroidery of this kind was in England during the thirteenth century. Church vestments made were of such excellent design and workmanship that they were exported all over the then known world. Called "Opus Anglicanum," or English work, the embroidery was done in a stitch called "couché rentré," or "pulled couching." (See page 43.) One of the most beautiful examples of Opus Anglicanum is the Syon Cope, now in the Victoria and Albert Museum. Worked in the twelfth century, probably for Coventry, it was ultimately given to the convent at Syon near London. The gray stone of Syon House rises above the rush-grown banks of the Thames at Isleworth, so often swathed in river mists. Against this background one can visualize the Syon Cope gleaming like an antique jewel, its muted colors intertwined with glints of silver and gold, the medieval panoply of its design telling the uninitiated its story without words. The central panel shows the Crucifixion of Christ. Radiating from it are scenes from his life. Between each scene are the seraphim with peacock feather wings: "with twain they did cover their face, with twain they did cover their feet, with twain they did fly."

But apart from its ecclesiastical use in the Middle Ages, embroidery with silk and gold thread was imparting a luxury to secular life. Chaucer wrote:

> I woll gyve him a fetherbed
> Rayed with golde and ryght well cled
> In fyne black sattin doutrmere
> And many a pylow and everybere
> Of cloth of raynes to sleppe on softe
> Hym there not nede to turn ofte.

Details from the Syon Cope: Doubting Thomas and St. Michael (below). *Victoria and Albert Museum*

Jupon of the Black Prince. *Canterbury Cathedral*

LEFT

Tomb cover of John, the son of Basil Lupu (the wolf), from Jassy, capital of Moldavia. Worked in 1650, with faces in applied silk and features in stitchery; the flowers and border designs show Persian influence

Herald's tabard of the Lord Lyon King of Arms. *Victoria and Albert Museum*

We can visualize the richness of these textiles when we know how equally magnificent the background fabrics were: damask from Damascus; velvet, an ancient material which was originally called fustian; baudekin, an Eastern fabric shot with gold, much used behind royal thrones—these were just a few of the many beautiful ones. Thomas of Woodstock, Duke of Gloucester, had listed in his inventory, "A large bed of blue baudekyn embroidered with silver owls and gold fleurs de lys" and another bed of "black baudekyn powdered with white roses."

The noble ladies were striking figures at this time, too, we are told. The clergy upbraided them and called them "foxes, whose only care is the ornament of their long tails," and condemned all these "crimple-crispings and christy-crosties and gold thread." But Byzantium was really the center of everything. As Diehl says, "The entire world, under the cold fogs of the north, by the long Russian rivers, in the counting houses of Venice and the castles of the West, dreamed of Byzantium as an incomparable city, unique in the world: all shining in a glittering radiance of gold." Sumptuous fabrics, tents of cloth of gold—Arabian and Jewish writers have said they were unable to describe the grandeur of the city—"The motley splendor of the streets filled with people so beautifully arrayed they all resemble the children of the king!"

Through the ancient trade routes, whose very names summon up visions—from the Euphrates and the Oxus rivers to the Caspian Sea, Antioch, Aden, and Palmyra—Byzantium influenced the whole of Western art. The most important part of its commerce with Germany, Bulgaria and Hungary, Venice and the Levant were textiles and embroidery. A description of the Egyptian caliphs' court at this time sounds just like the *Arabian Nights.* "The carpets of this noble saloon consisted of one piece of cloth-of-gold embroidered with bunches of roses in red and white silk; and the dome, painted in the same manner, after the Arabian fashion, presented to the mind one of the most charming objects. In every space between the columns was a little sofa adorned in the same manner . . . and looking out on the most delicious garden, the walks of which were of little pebbles of different colors, of the same pattern as the carpet of the saloon; so that looking upon the carpet within and without, it seemed as if the dome and the garden with all its ornaments had been upon the same carpet."

The splendor of needlework combined with sumptuous velvets,

cloth of gold, and gleaming silks was never more brilliantly shown than when it was used for heraldry. Created in the twelfth century, although its ancestry can be traced from Egypt, Greece, and Rome, heraldry was a language invented to give instant recognition of their knights and leaders to the fighting men in battle.

The crest, like the feathered headdresses of the North American Indians, was the most conspicuous and obvious insignia. Worn above the completely closed and visored helm, it was indeed necessary for identification. But the gleaming suits of armor had the serious disadvantage of rusting in the rain, or worse, on crusades under a fierce Eastern sun, of broiling the warrior within. Therefore, the surcoat or jupon was designed. Worn over the armor, this textile covering not only acted as insulation, it could be embroidered with the owner's crest—hence the expression coat-of-arms. To this day the jupon of Edward the Black Prince (see page 10) hangs over his tomb in Canterbury Cathedral, where it has hung for five hundred years. It was embroidered in gold threads on red and blue velvet, or fustian. The velvet was backed on wool and linen and the whole coat was quilted together.

It is interesting to compare it with the herald's tabard (shown on the same page), made in the seventeenth century for the Lord Lyon King of Arms, since so many of the techniques are similar.

One of the finest examples of this elegant gold and silk work is a horse's lavish trappings with a fascinating and well-traveled history.

Part of the horse-trappings of John of Eltham, 14th century. *Musée de Cluny*

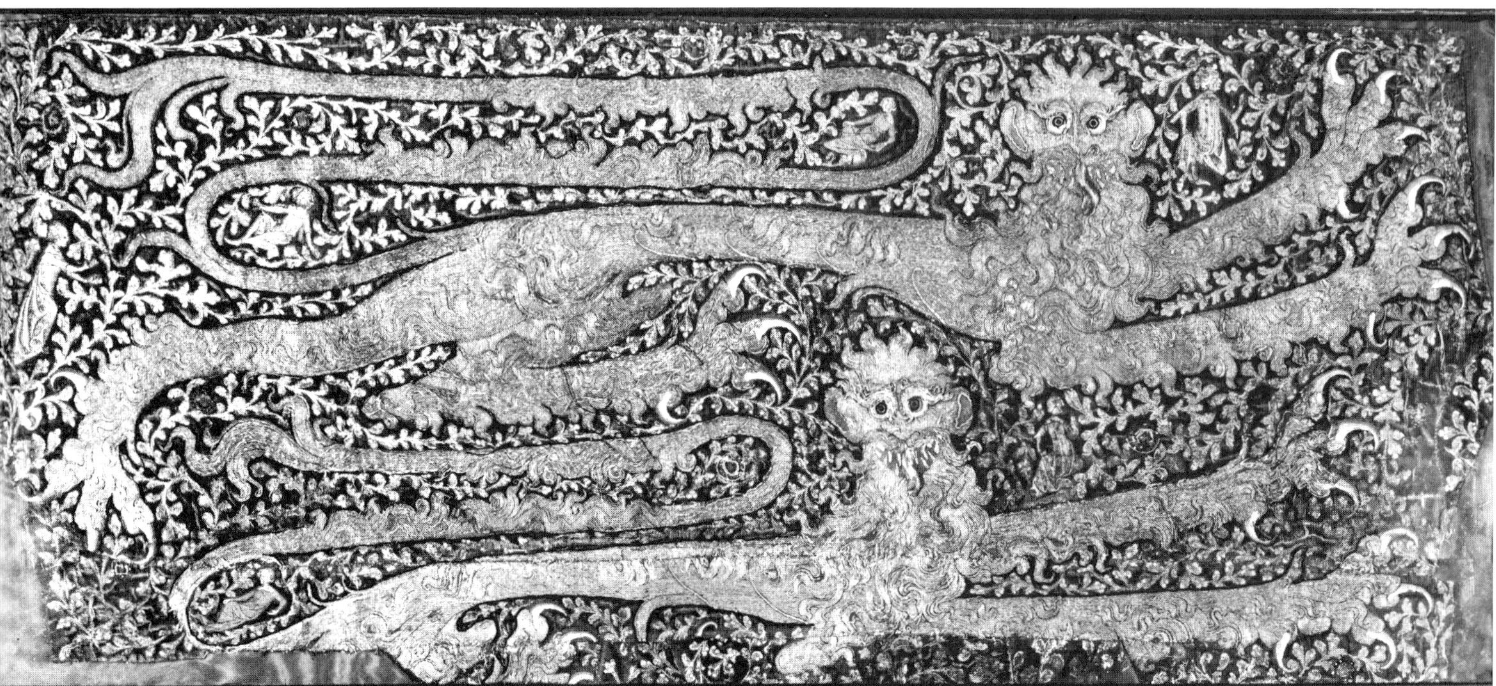

Imagine John of Eltham, second son of Edward II, galloping across the English countryside to his sister Eleanor's wedding in 1332, a glorious, awesome sight, straight from the pages of Sir Walter Scott. Even John's charger was caparisoned in fine Eastern velvet, very plush and blood-red. The three lions passant of England were embroidered with such detail on the stuff, every tawny hair was laid down with a fine gold thread. Even the full curling eyebrows were sewn in relief and the scarlet-rimmed black eyes flashed with crystal disks. Their sharp claws were raised and worked over in azure silk. The ground was so gorgeously grown with gold and silk vines that at first glance embroidered figures of men and women cannot be distinguished from the swirling foliage. (See opposite page.)

John either lost this greatly admired work in a tournament or extravagantly gave it away, but somehow the trappings reached foreign hands. They next appeared as a set of church vestments, the chasuble formed from the major part of the surcoat minus one of the lions. Finally they passed into private hands and are now in the collection of the Musée de Cluny in Paris.

Heraldic insignia and religious design served the same purpose—to communicate at a glance and without words—and all through the ages it is fascinating to observe the exchange of ecclesiastical vestments for secular use, and vice versa. Sometimes the church seemed to be in the ascendancy and magnificently embroidered hangings would be made into copes, chasubles, or altar frontals. At other times, generally in days of lesser prosperity, religious embroideries would be cut up for other purposes. During the eighteenth century, embroideries in metal were even assiduously pulled apart by ladies taking afternoon tea. "Drizzling," as it was called, became a fashionable pastime and many beautiful pieces of needlework were destroyed so that the gold and silver threads could be sold and melted down.

Compared with the splendor and lavish use of silk and gold thread in China, India, and Europe, the rather primitive rural life of the American countryside seemed more suited to the rougher texture of homespun and wool. At the beginning of the eighteenth century the "Gentleman's Progress" or the "itinerarium" of Dr. Alexander Hamilton shows how travel in the New World was indeed an adventure.

Man's vest. *Cooper Hewitt Museum of Design, Smithsonian Institution*

Dress elaborately embroidered with silver gilt and silk, early 18th century. *Victoria and Albert Museum*

Detail of man's vest. *Colonial Williamsburg*

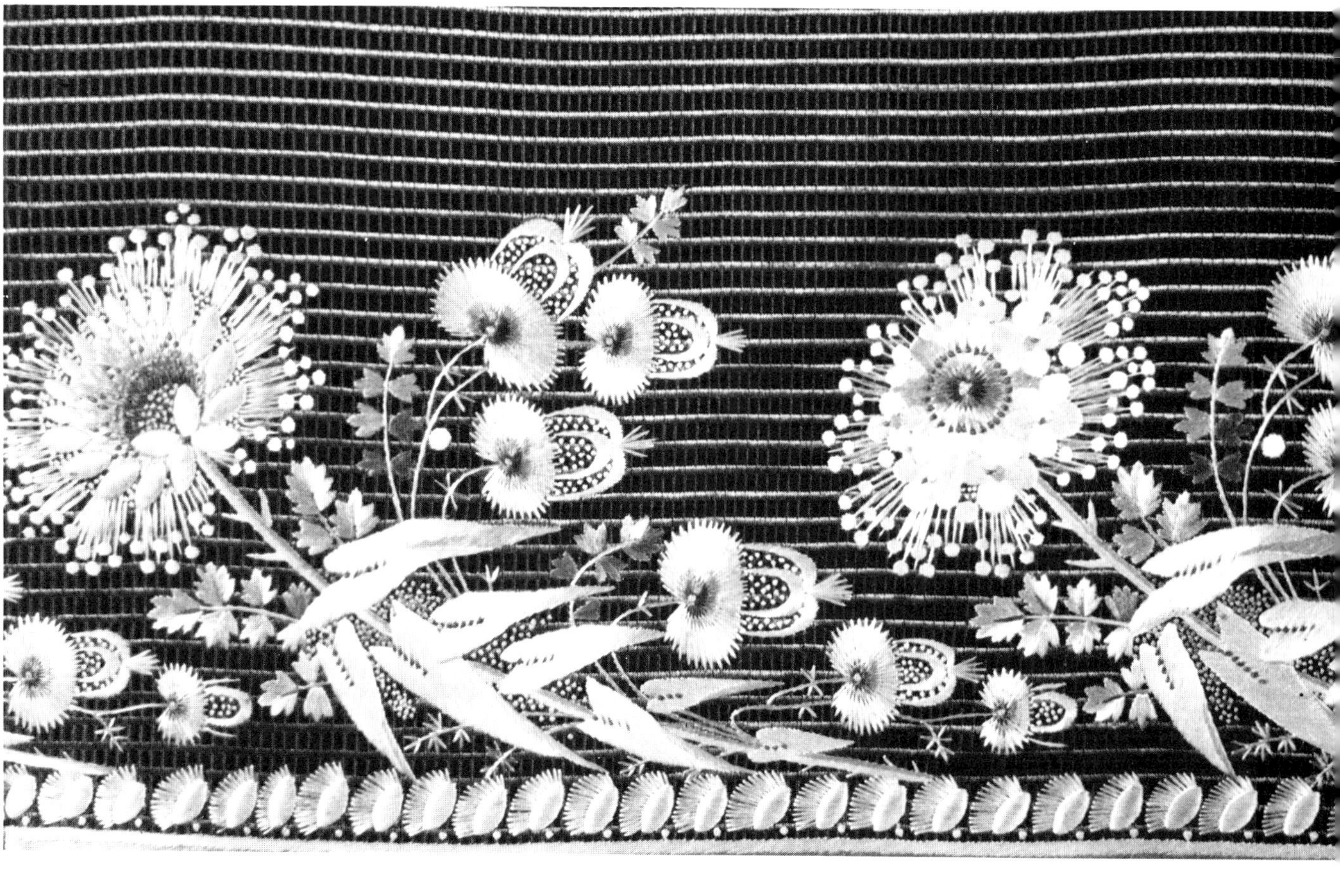

> We took horse again (from Setauket) att half an hour after 5 o'clock and had scarce got a mile when we lost our way—after riding ten miles thro woods and marshes in which we were pestered by muscettos, we arrived at 8 o'clock att night att one Brewsters where we put up for all night and in this house we could get nothing either to eat or drink and so were obliged to go to bed fasting or supperless.
>
> The people in this house seemed to be quite savage and rude.
>
> When I waked this morning I found two beds in the room besides that in which I lay, in one of which lay two great hulking fellows with long black beards, having their own hair and not as much as half a night cap betwixt them both.
>
> I took them for Weavers, not only from their greasy appearance, but because I observed a weaver's loom at each side of the room.
>
> We set out from this desolate place att 6 o'clock and rid 16 miles thro very barren and waste land.

The Colonial housewife naturally used those materials closest at hand—worsteds and crewels—to interpret in needlework those things which were a fascinating part of her new world: deer, wild turkey, beaver, raccoons and gray squirrels, peach orchards, wild grapes, and fields of watermelons or pumpkins. Meanwhile the Atlantic was well traveled by ships of the East India Company, laden with rare fabrics from Teheran and Samarkand, costly perfumes, spices, ointments, and precious woods. It was inevitable that privateers and freebooters should be tempted by this booty and, plying their trade through Madagascar, the pirates ultimately conveyed it to New York. Thus New York in turn became a city of almost oriental magnificence, peopled by such colorful characters as Thomas Tew, who arrived in 1694 with great wealth from the Indian seas. He was a "slight dark man of about forty, who dressed richly and scattered gold profusely. His uniform was a blue cap with a band of cloth of silver. His blue jacket was bordered with gold lace, and further garnished with large pearl buttons. Loose trunks of white linen covered his lower limbs as far as the knee, where they gave place to curiously worked stockings. A rich chain of Arabian gold hung from his neck, and through the meshes of a curiously knit belt gleamed a dagger, its hilt set with the rarest of gems. This person, dispensing draughts of sopus ale to whoever would drink, and throwing golden louis d'or about as carelessly as though they were stuyvers, soon became a familiar object in the streets and taverns of New York."

The city, like a miniature London, but more cosmopolitan, became a center of fashion for silk and embroidered clothing, infinite in its variety and exquisite in its coloring and fine stitchery. "Broadway on a Sabbath morning, as the bells were ringing for church, must then have presented an animated and ever brilliant spectacle, for both ladies and gentlemen shone rich as emperor moths."

Imagine Nicholas Bayard, secretary of the province and colonel of the militia, wearing a cinnamon-colored cloth coat—embroidered four or five inches deep with silver and lined with sky blue silk, with breeches to match, dove-colored silk stockings, and shoes with silver buckles. He takes snuff and afterward applies to his nose a silk handkerchief embroidered with the arms of Britain. His wife, rivaling this magnificence, wears purple and gold silk over black velvet edged with silver, with green silk stockings and shoes of fine morocco leather embroidered with red clocks.

Queen Charlotte's bedspread, colored silk flowers on white satin quilted with gold thread. *Victoria and Albert Museum*

Panel from a dress shown at the Paris Exhibition, 1851 (see sketch). Padded satin in brilliant reds, blues, greens, and cream silk, on caramel taffeta. *Author's Collection*

An increased elegance in furnishings as well as dress was inspired by London fashions, though William Smith, a resident historian, observed, "by the time we adopt them they become disused in England."

Toward the end of the eighteenth century in England silk almost completely superseded wool for embroidery on bed furnishings and household articles as well as clothing, though in America some silk thread was sold from door to door by pedlars, crewel was continuously popular until the end of the century.

During the Victorian era the designs for embroidery in both countries became rather heavy and serious. Everything was overspread with needlework, antimacassars, bureau scarves, wall pockets; even meat safes and beaded milk-jug covers were considered suitable subjects for silken stitchery. The mantelpiece was covered, and even the piano was not allowed to show its legs: over it would be thrown a deeply fringed shawl,

Detail from William Morris hand-blocked linen. *Victoria and Albert Museum*

or a closely stitched "table carpet" often worked in the favorite predominating colors of black, deep maroon, or filthy green!

A man who had profound influence on Victorian design, however, was William Morris, who established a factory that produced hand-blocked linens, wallpapers, and embroideries. His designs, stemming from the influence of oriental stylization of natural forms, really transcended the more mundane ones then in vogue and led the way to the graceful flowing lines of art nouveau. His gentle admonition to the Victorian embroideress is good to remember in any age and at any time.

"Now indeed it is a delightful idea to cover a piece of linen cloth with roses, and jonquils, and tulips, all done quite natural with the needle, and we can't go too far in that direction if we only remember the nature of our craft in general; and since we are using specially beautiful materials, that we shall make the most of them, and not forget that we are gardening with silk and gold thread."

TO BEGIN

With sophisticated gold threads and silken stitches you can create almost anything from a wall panel to a family coat of arms, an altar frontal to a mirror frame, an evening dress, a handbag, or even a devastating vest or cummerbund for a peacock husband.

Don't think that you must be restricted to rigid rules and concepts, or that because gold and silk are together in this book you must use them that way forever. In Queen Anne's time in England, for instance, silk was combined with wool in the transition from Jacobean to all-silk embroideries.

One thing leads to another, and once you have experimented with the stitches and begun to be familiar with the exciting techniques, ideas will crop up like daisies and you will develop your own individual approach to the medium. The easiest way to explore some of the fascinating possibilities is to make a sampler using the traditional threads as well as some of the many new ones. Design the sampler with simple shapes so that you can fill in areas with different methods and stitches, but make it attractive enough to hang as a wall panel; it seems a pity to spend valuable time on something that is to be hidden in a bottom drawer.

RIGHT
Blanket cover for a child's crib, all white silk, with blue collar, on white wool background. Shading effect is achieved by simply following the outlines with rows of split stitch. *Designed and worked by Mrs. Joseph Berger*

BELOW
Pillow from Gracie Mansion, designed by the author for Mrs. John Lindsay, worked by Mrs. Hampton Lynch, silk and wool on gold Scalamandré silk

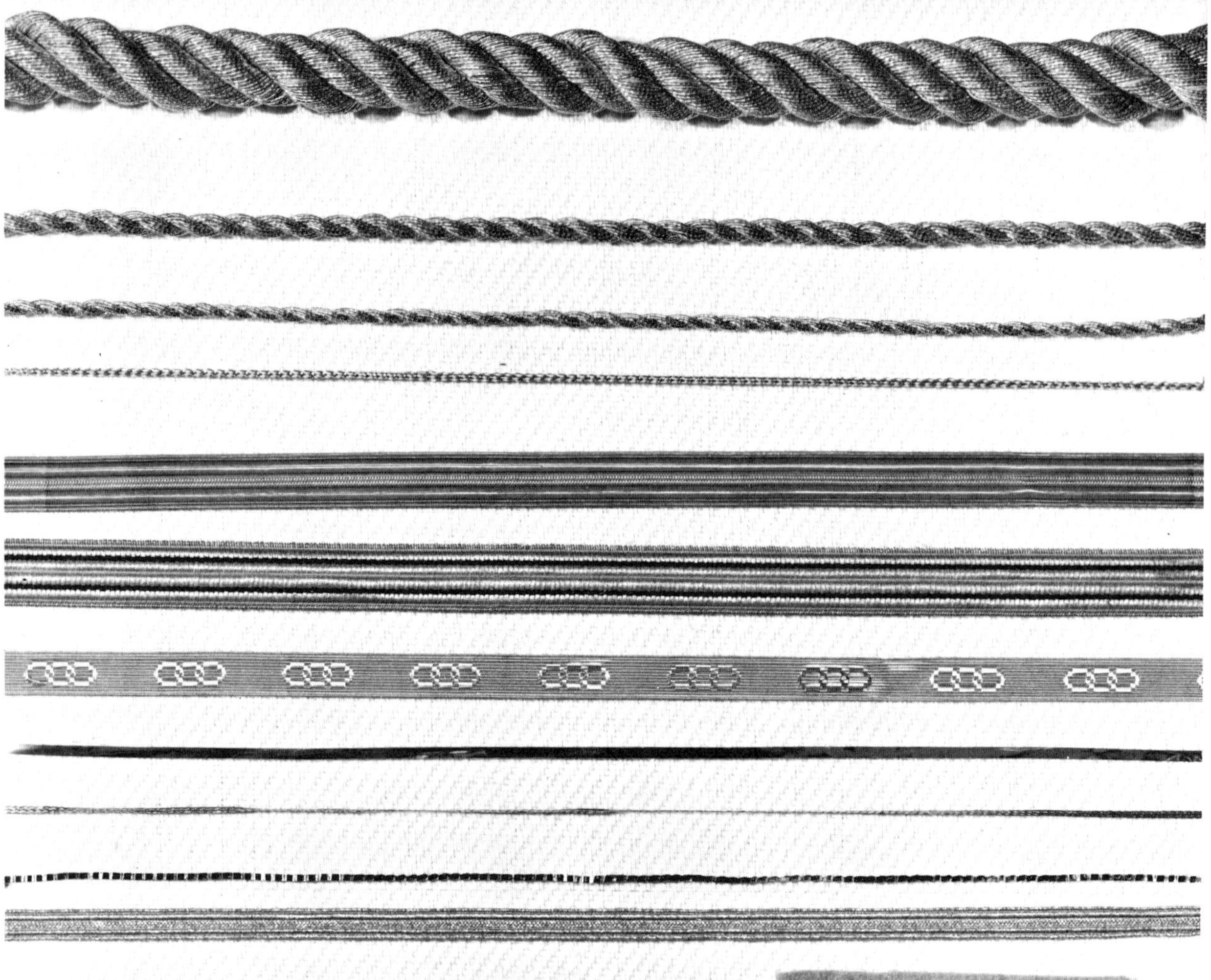

Twisted cords and flat braids; bottom right, bullion threads of different sizes being cut

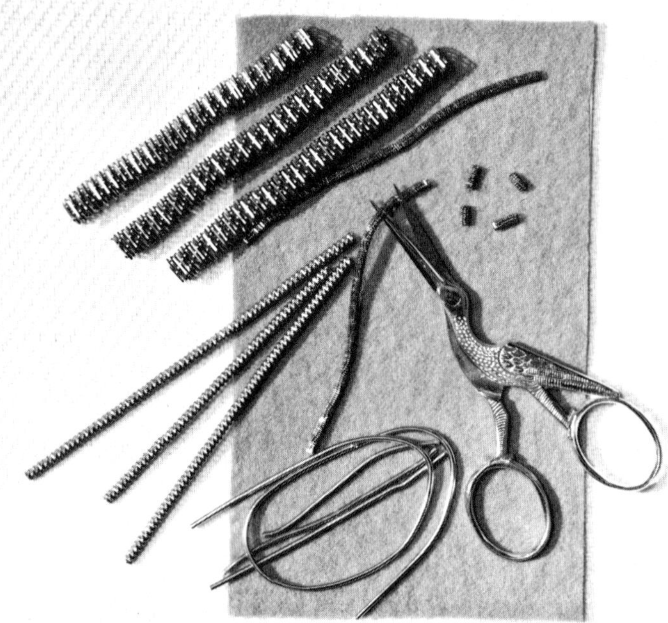

Blazer pocket, showing Nantucket yacht club badge in gold bullion

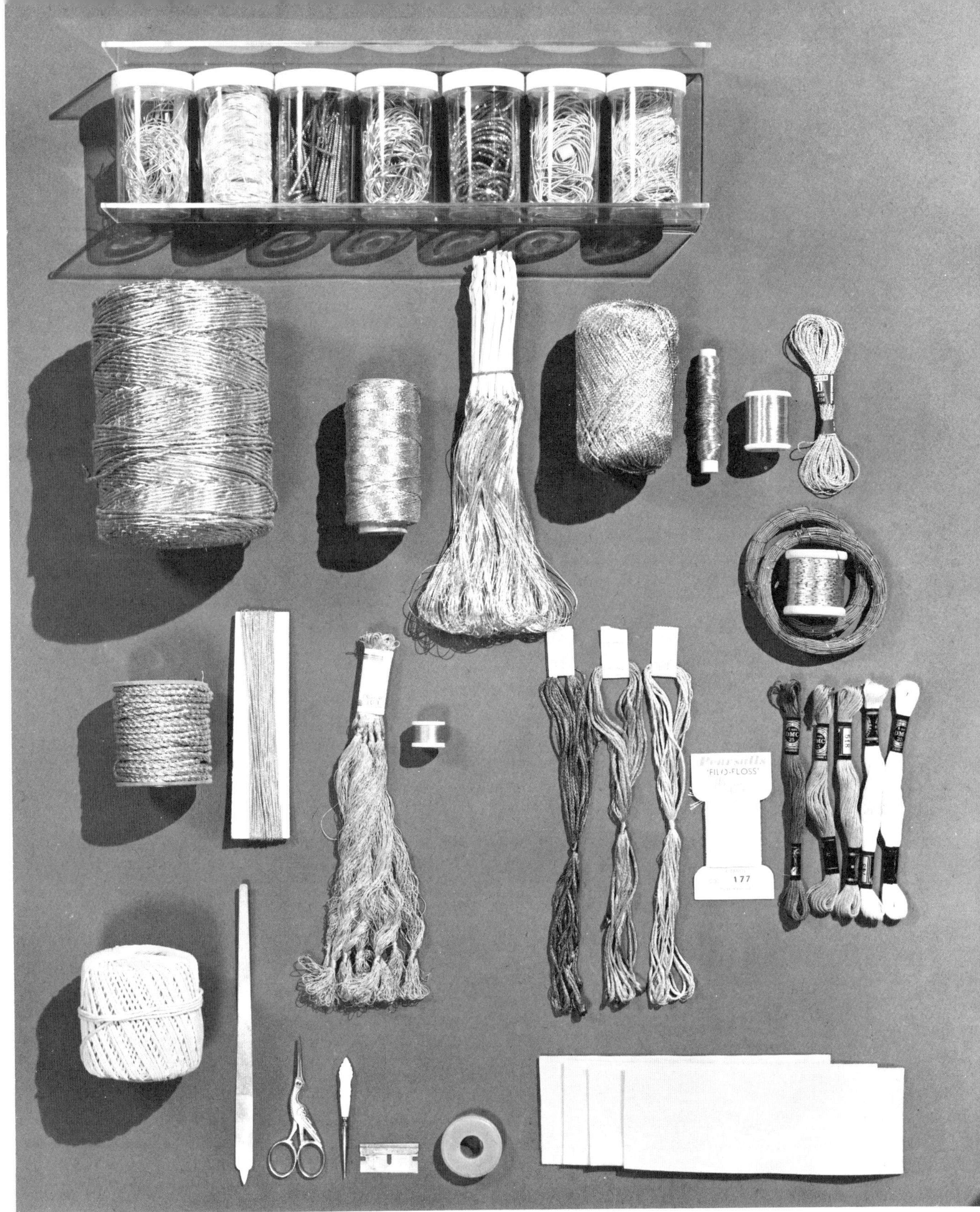

TOP. Various bullion threads
2ND ROW. Imitation Japanese gold thread, heavy and medium; real Japanese gold; Lurex knitting thread; fine Lurex sewing threads; spool of "plate," a flat metal for couching
3RD ROW. Gold cords, heavy and fine; Maltese sewing silk or "horsetail"; Filo floss; DMC cotton
BOTTOM. String for padding; nail file (for pushing gold into place when couching), scissors, stiletto, razor blade, and beeswax; felt for padding

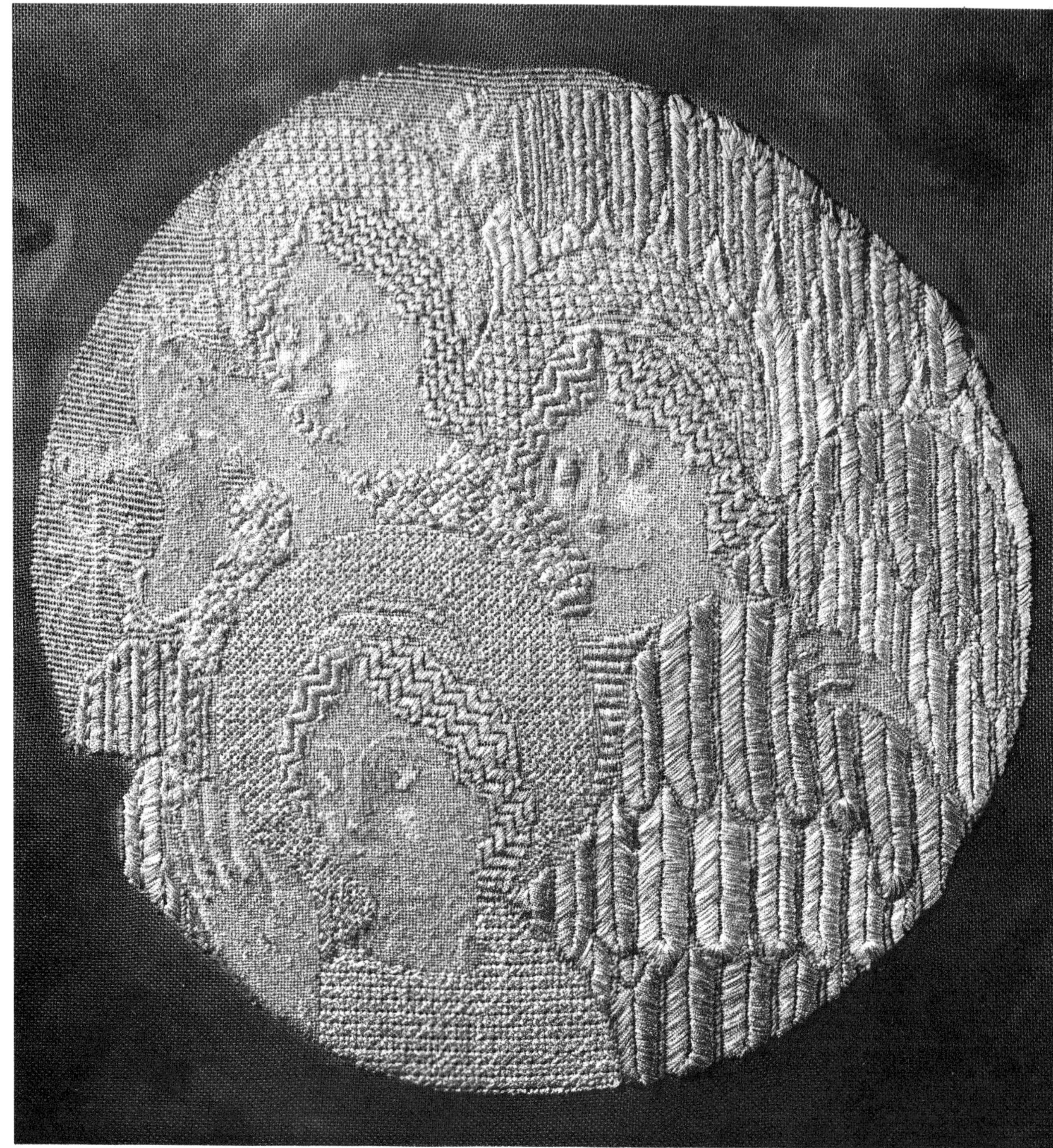

Needlepoint stitches in Lurex on canvas; embroidery and open canvas around it were painted with brown oil paint. *Designed and worked by Robert Heitmann*

COLLECTING THE THREADS

SILK AND COTTON THREADS

Silk and cotton threads can be used in exactly the same way as you use crewel wool but, of course, with more delicate results. Real silk threads may be hard to find, although they are available in various forms, both as floss or twisted like a fine cord (Pearsall's Filo Floss and Filoselle Silk). However, cotton makes a good substitute, and the mercerized embroidery floss and various types of crochet cotton available in all the stores, though not as soft as real silk, wear better, come in a good range of colors, and may sometimes be scarcely distinguishable from silk itself. Besides this, embroidery floss has the advantage of being washable, is ideal for clothing, and is versatile enough to be as thoroughly at home on a blue denim work shirt as on a black satin cummerbund or evening vest. The stitches can also add a variety of effects, lacy when worked openly; or when worked closely—using stitches such as padded satin—becoming vibrant and shiny as enamel. Silk, cotton, and wool are really completely interchangeable. The only thing that sets cotton or silk apart is its finer scale and smoother texture. Therefore, any of the stitches described in crewel embroidery may be worked in silk or cotton.

LUREX THREADS

The soft pliable gold or silver Lurex threads can also be handled like silk or wool with crewel stitches. When they are fine enough, they may be stitched right through the fabric, using a large crewel or chenille needle to protect them from tearing. St. George and the Dragon (page 25) was done with a variety of flat and open-patterned crewel stitches combined with solid filling stitches on a silk background. All kinds of Lurex can be used effectively on needlepoint canvas, too, as in the Singing Angels on the opposite page.

METAL THREADS

Real gold and metal threads, and occasionally some types of Lurex, need special treatment. They are either too wiry or too delicate to sew right through the fabric, and so have to be sewn down on the surface. These special techniques come into play when you embroider with such threads as Japanese gold and use romantic-sounding materials such as gold bullion, pearl purl, and plate. The beauty of Japanese gold is that it will never tarnish; it maintains its original gleaming depth of mellow color year after year. This is because it is made of pure gold leaf on narrow strips of paper lightly coiled around a core of orange or yellow silk.

Bullion is a wire thread coiled like a tight spring and is therefore hollow in the center. Unlike a spring, however, it will not snap back into place after being stretched out, so you have to handle it very carefully. Because of its fragility it is generally cut into short lengths, and each one is sewn down like a bead onto the fabric, using a waxed thread for strength.

Bullion thread comes in three varieties. The first, "rough" or "matte" (to give both the English and French names), has a dull satin sheen. The second, "smooth" or "glissant," is a shinier gleaming bullion, and the third, "check" or "frisé," is a crinkled variety with a sparkling effect.

If these threads seem very foreign and remote to you, just look closely again at a club or army badge on a hat, blazer, or uniform. You will realize that you have often seen them before—the raised insignia which go back to the beginning of heraldry (see page 20) and are still used today. These are the threads which constitute the "scrambled eggs" on the naval officer's hat, or are used to embroider the identifying burgee of a yacht club on a blazer jacket. They would be equally effective used on a box top, for a mirror frame, for a very special evening bag, or for your own family coat of arms.

Most of the stores carry the metal threads put out by knitting wool manufacturers, so that notions departments and variety stores are the places to start looking for gold and silver threads. But all through the year and especially at Christmastime you may find different tinsel threads in the gift stores, and all kinds of cords and braids in the gift wrapping departments. Since these are nearly always Lurex they will not tarnish and can be used most effectively. As the demand grows, so will the number of places where real gold threads are available. The best thing to do is to amass a collection of metal threads to choose from, buying them wherever and whenever you see them, so that you can select the most suitable for a particular design as you work.

St. George and the Dragon, all gold threads stitched on red damask. *Designed and worked by Mrs. Hugh M. Parrish*

CHOOSING FABRICS

There is almost no limit to the types of material you can work on, but fine linen is probably the easiest to begin with. However, if you want to work with fairly heavy gold thread on delicate white taffeta, for instance, or with fine silk on a rather stretchy open weave linen, you will find that you must back them first with another material such as lightweight linen or muslin; otherwise they will pucker. First baste the two pieces of material smoothly, together, so that they become as one. Then embroider the design by working through both layers of fabric, and when the embroidery is finished, cut away the backing material around the stitches on the wrong side.

Velvet is the most difficult material to work on, because when you transfer the design, the pile often shifts, causing the design to be placed inaccurately. Then, when you take the stitches, the pile sometimes flattens itself in some places and not in others, giving an untidy look. This limits

TOP LEFT TO RIGHT. Antique velvet, slubbed silk, rayon damask, striped upholstery satin
2ND ROW. Silk damask, wool-backed upholstery satin (matte finish), linen
3RD ROW. Cotton velvet, ribbed cotton, brushed nylon, blue denim

the stitches that can easily be done to couching, padded satin, and laid work, because these seem to lie most smoothly in the pile. One way to avoid all this is to do what was done in the fourteenth century: to overlay the whole velvet on top with fine linen or muslin with the design traced on it, embroider through both layers, and then cut away the linen from the front—very closely around the design.

Thus you can see that almost any fabric can be converted so that it is suitable for use with silk and gold threads. Not only this, but the traditional idea that rich and sumptuous threads should always be worked on equally magnificent background fabrics which harmonize with them has given way to a different approach of surprise contrasts. Today it is possible to choose rough wool or even homespun linen or cotton as a background for fine silk and gold embroidery, or to combine silk, gold, *and* wool when working on damask or brocade.

White silk on dove-colored velvet

THE TOOLS OF THE TRADE

Now that you have found your silk and metal threads, you will need to collect a few other things before you can launch into your stitching.

First, *needles.* You will need a varied assortment, because you will be working with threads of such different thicknesses. Become like a squirrel and hoard in your workbox packets of needles which you buy whenever you come across them. Sometimes needles of the right size are very hard to find. Should they become rusty, rub them with fine sandpaper, or run them in and out of one of those little strawberry pincushions filled with emery powder.

Next, you must find silk or *mercerized cotton* for couching down the metal threads. The best for the purpose is a Maltese sewing silk, known as Horsetail, which is very strong and fine, and comes in two shades of yellow and silver gray. Any thread you use must be fine enough not to detract from the metal, and therefore must be waxed for strength.

Most notion stores have *beeswax.* This is necessary for protecting the fine silk or cotton so that it will not be cut by the metal threads when it is used to sew them down. Thread the needle and draw the silk two or three times through the beeswax before sewing with it. The wax stiffens the thread, too, making it easier to handle. Candlewax will do, but is not quite so "clingy."

A *stiletto* should be possible to find at a sewing or notion store, too, but a large chenille or pointed rug needle will do if a stiletto is not available. The stiletto is used for opening a hole in the background material, so that the extra thick ends of couched metal threads may be easily taken through to the reverse side.

You will need *felt* (of medium thickness) for padding. If you are going to cover it with gold thread, buy yellow or orange, because although it won't actually show, minute areas which are not covered influence the color of the metal thread. For silver threads, use pale blue felt. *String* is also used for padding. The best kind is not a twisted cord, but a waxed string which is smooth and firm. An average size string is #30. Anything finer than this will not raise the threads sufficiently to make an effect.

BEGINNING THE DESIGN

If you are starting with a sampler, you may get some inspiration from the wild arum lily on page 38, used to illustrate the basic stitches, or the design used to show the techniques of flat and raised couching, page 47. Alternatively, you may want to start out with a belt or handbag, or, perhaps, undaunted, launch right into making a large hanging. In any case, if you have the design, the threads, the background fabric, and the tools at hand, your next step will be to stretch the material in a frame. If your background fabric is stretched out taut, it will be much easier to take accurate, smooth stitches when handling the wiry gold threads. Since many silk materials, particularly satin, show a ring if you use an embroidery hoop, and since the gold threads would obviously be damaged if a hoop were forced over them, an artist's square frame is the best to use. You *can* work on any oval rug hoop, if the design will fit within it, but be sure the fabric which is to show will not be marked by the outer hoop.

APPLYING THE PATTERN

To be successful, traditional gold and silk embroidery must be precise and accurate. Therefore, design placement is better done on fabric that is stretched taut in a square frame rather than by the normal method of holding it flat on a table with masking tape.

To establish the center of your working area, and to give you straight guide lines for placing your design, baste contrasting colored threads through the middle of the fabric in your frame, vertically and horizontally. If you are working on linen, do this by using a blunt needle and work between the threads of the fabric, following them to keep your stitches straight. If you are working on finer fabric, use a ruler. Mark the line with pins first, and follow this with a basting line sewn with a sharp needle. Place your frame over some books, records, or any firm working surface, so that the material in the frame does not sag as you lean on it, and transfer the design to the fabric by the most suitable method on pages 30–33.

All this preparation may seem like a great deal of trouble at first, but it will be worth it in the long run. Following the correct method really saves a good deal of time and effort later on.

APPLYING THE DESIGN

Whether you draw your own original design or whether you adapt a pattern, it really takes no more skill to put your own design on fabric than it does to embroider the stitches. The following are some simple methods. You will be able to choose which method is best according to the texture of fabric you are working on. For smooth materials that are light in color the following is the quickest way of transferring the design.

APPLYING THE DESIGN WITH DRESSMAKERS' CARBON

Buy a packet of dressmakers' carbon from any notions department or sewing supply shop. (Ordinary carbon will smudge.) Fold the material in half and then in half again, and crease the folds so that they show clearly. Then smooth the material flat on a table or board and hold it down evenly with masking tape on all four sides (as shown). A really smooth hard surface is necessary.

Fold the design, too, into four equal parts, open it up, and lay it down on top. Now slide a sheet of carbon paper, face downward, between paper and material. Use blue carbon for light materials, white for dark ones. Anchor the paper with some heavy weights (books, paperweights, etc.) and trace round the outline *very heavily* with

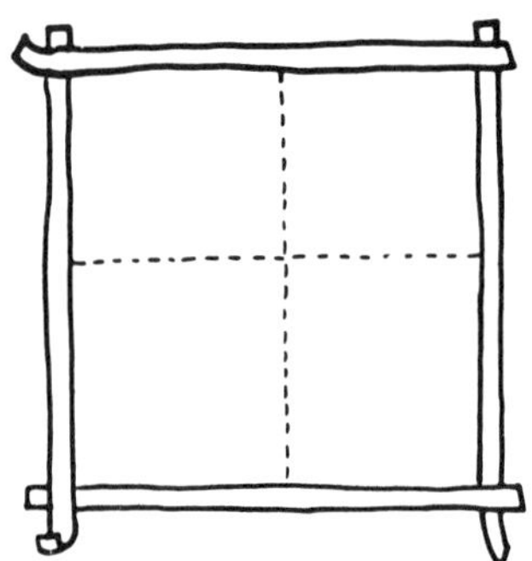

Having folded the material, lay it out and fasten down with masking tape.

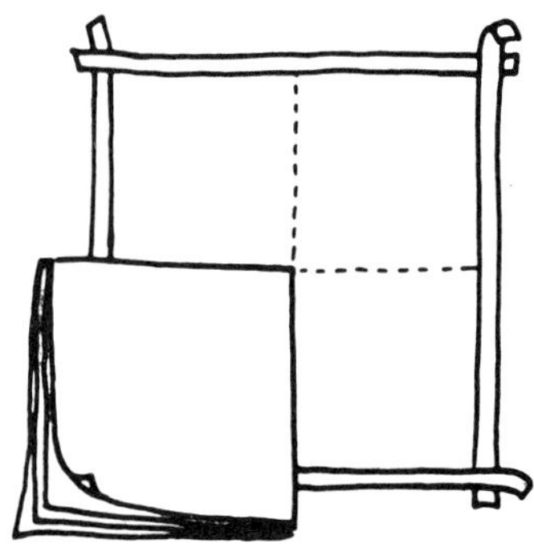

Fold the design into four parts and place it in position on one quarter of the fabric.

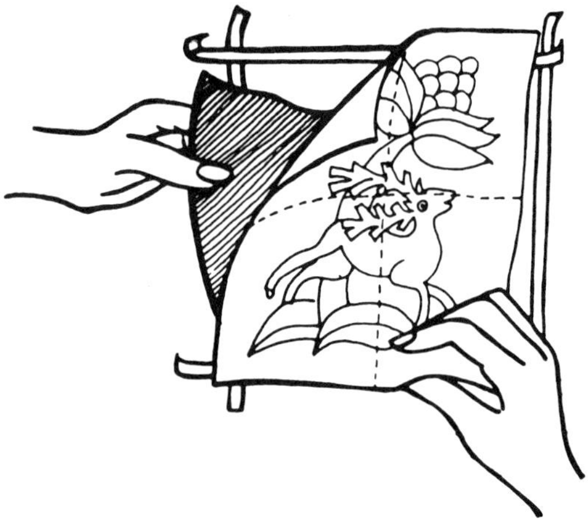

Slide the carbon paper, face down, under the design, being careful not to shift the paper out of position.

a pencil. Using weights is a better idea than taping the design all round, because you can lift a corner occasionally to see how well the carbon is transferring. You really must *engrave* heavily to get good results, but you will soon find this out as you work.

APPLYING THE DESIGN WITH BASTING STITCHES

Buy some batiste, organdy, or chiffon, and trace the design through the transparent material, using a hard pencil. (Of course the first two methods may also be used for this equally well, if desired.)

Pin the material with the design to the wrong side of the fabric. Then baste all around the outlines with small running stitches, using a contrasting color thread. The design will then be transferred onto the right side, and may be embroidered right over the running stitches to cover them.

Another method of transferring a design onto materials such as silk, velvets, and dark or delicate fabrics is:

APPLYING THE DESIGN WITH TRACING PAPER

This method is also excellent for ties and sweaters, or anything that you might be afraid of damaging if you put the design on incorrectly. With tracing or tissue paper any mistakes can be ripped out, leaving no sign of any unwanted design on the fabric!

First trace your design onto tracing paper or, even better, soft pliable tissue, using a felt-tipped pen which is soft and will not tear the paper. Center it, pin it, and then baste it into position on the material. Embroider the design, working through the paper and the fabric together. It is best to do the embroidery on a frame, or the paper may get damaged as you work. When you have finished, tear the tissue away, and, *voilà*—there is your design revealed on the cloth, looking beautiful! With your needle, stroke out any little pieces of paper left between the stitching.

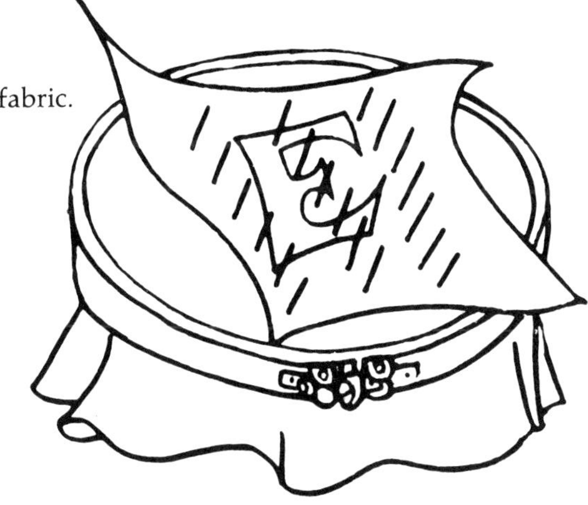

Design on tracing paper basted in place on fabric.

APPLYING THE DESIGN WITH NET

If your fabric is very "knubbly" and rough textured, and your design is bold in scale, use this method to transfer the pattern directly on the cloth. Trace the design onto regular net, using a rather heavy black permanent marker. Then pin the net in position on the cloth and trace it again, using the marking pen. The ink from the pen will pass through the holes of the net to the cloth, giving you a clear outline which is easy to follow. Adjust the thickness of your felt-tipped marking pen to the texture of the material.

Last but not least, perhaps you may want to let your stitches dictate your pattern, and not be regulated by any permanent lines on the cloth, yet need some guide lines to help you. In this case you can try the following method.

APPLYING THE DESIGN FREEHAND

Since you need only a rough suggestion of the pattern and not a detailed drawing, you have several choices. You can mark your design with blackboard or tailor's chalk, which will rub off whenever you want to remove it . . . and sometimes before, which is one of its disadvantages! To make more definite, clearer lines you could lightly mark the fabric with a watercolor felt-tipped pen, and then wash the fabric afterward if any unwanted lines are showing. (However, be sure first to test your fabric for washability.)

Another method you could try is to baste the lines with contrasting color thread, which can be removed afterward. Alternatively, and this is really freehand, you can *stroke* the fabric as it is held taut in the frame, using a blunt needle. This method is used by quilters who outline each shape of their pattern as they work. Let the needle follow your hand, holding it almost parallel to the surface of the stretched material as you stroke firmly. A clear groove or crease will be formed. If it is done carefully it will not tear the fabric, yet the creased lines will be clear enough to follow, and will fade away when not wanted.

TRANSFERRING A GEOMETRIC PATTERN TO FINE MATERIAL

To embroider cross stitch or any geometric design on fabric that does not have a clearly defined weave, baste a piece of single weave

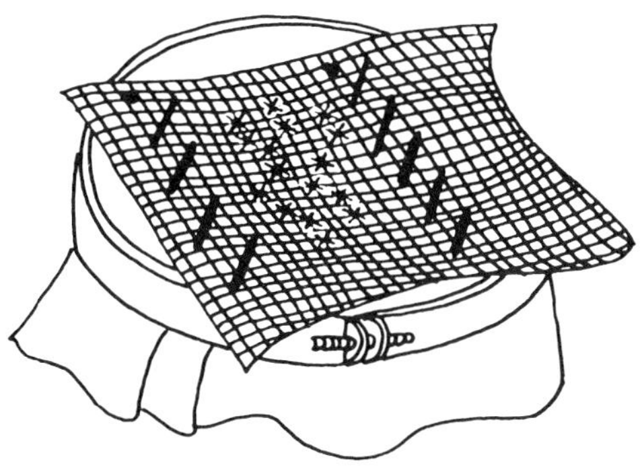

Applying a geometric pattern:
Cross stitch being worked through both canvas and background fabric

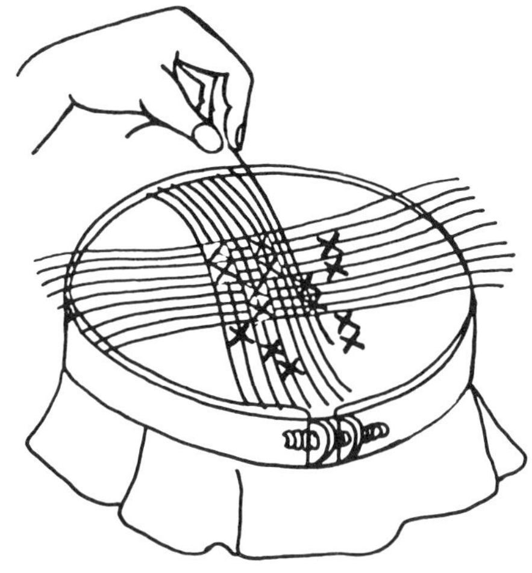

Canvas threads being pulled out when stitching is complete

needlepoint canvas (mono) over the area where the pattern is to be. Stretch the whole thing in an embroidery frame and stitch the pattern through both thicknesses, keeping your stitches even by counting the threads of the canvas. When the design is finished, unravel the threads of the canvas at the edges and draw them right out, one by one. If your fabric is washable it may be easier to do this if you soak the embroidery in cold water. This softens the sizing in the canvas and loosens the threads enough to allow them to slip out easily.

CHOOSING A FRAME

First of all, is a frame really necessary? The answer is yes! The stitches of any embroidery—crewel, silk, and needlepoint—are easier to keep neat and even as long as the background fabric is stretched taut. Hoops and ring frames are the most versatile way to stretch out the fabric because you can work on articles of any size. (If your design is on too small a piece of material, simply stitch strips of linen or sheeting to the four sides to extend the fabric.) A floor stand goes one step further because it allows you to have both hands free for working, which greatly increases your speed and skill. In fact once you are accustomed to using this type of frame, you will never want to be without it.

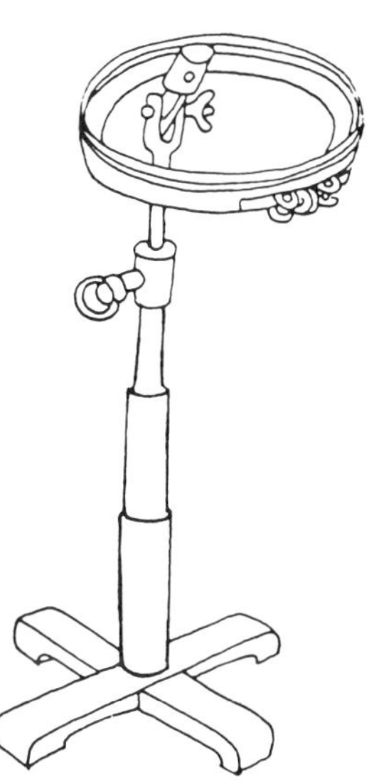

Standing floor frame

Lap or "fanny" frame

The only disadvantage of a standing frame is that you can't carry it around with you very easily, so a more portable variety is a lap frame, which has been nicknamed the "fanny frame" because you can sit on it! This makes it very firm and yet flexible to work on—and means you can do your embroidery almost anywhere—in the car, the plane, at the meeting, at the hairdresser's, the office, even in bed!

Linen or wool fabrics and needlepoint canvas are tough and resilient, and therefore never get damaged by having the hoops pushed over them. Certain delicate materials or raised stitches, however, might be marked by a hoop, so place layers of tissue paper over the design before pushing the frame down. Then tear the paper away from the surface of the work, leaving it protecting the fabric round the edge where the hoop would be liable to chafe it. Alternatively, you have four other choices. One is to mount a piece of linen into the ring frame, and then baste your fabric to the linen on top of the frame, just where the design area is. Work through both layers, and then cut the linen away on the reverse side, all around the design area.

The second choice is to use a large oval rug or quilting hoop (see illustration) so that the material that is marked by the hoop will only be at the outer edges, which will not show. (The oval hoop is also useful for large-scale embroidery of any kind.)

The third choice is to work on a stretcher frame. Artists' stretcher frames, used for oil painting, come in all sizes and are available from almost every art store. You should buy a larger size than the finished measurement of your work to allow you to work right up to the edge of the design without the wooden strips getting in your way. Assemble the four strips and stretch your material tightly over the frame, thumbtacking or stapling the fabric to the back. Then work exactly as you would on an embroidery hoop. When finished, if the design is to be a panel, you have an "instant picture" ready to hang on the wall! If the material becomes slack while you are working on it, push some thread or material into the sides to make it tight.

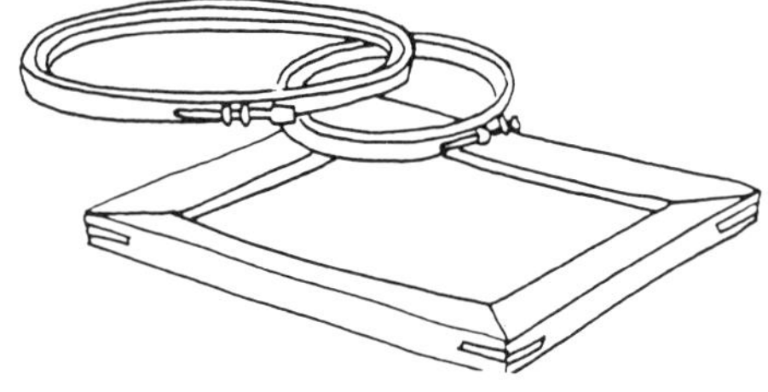

Embroidery hoops with adjustable screw; artists' stretcher frame

MOUNTING WORK IN A RING FRAME

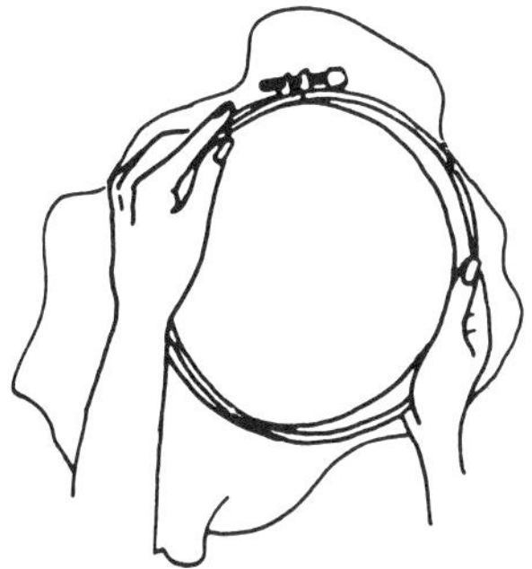

Before assembling the frame, adjust the screw so that the outer hoop fits snugly over the inner ring and the material. *Never* try to alter the screw when the frame is in place.

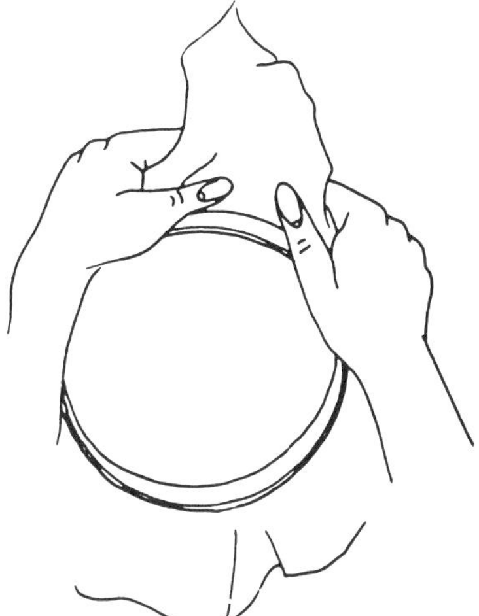

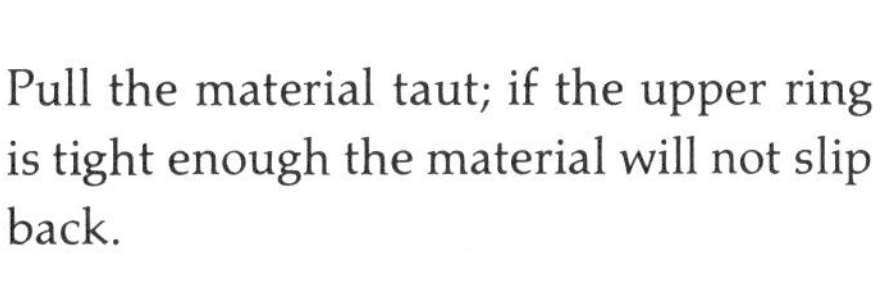

Pull the material taut; if the upper ring is tight enough the material will not slip back.

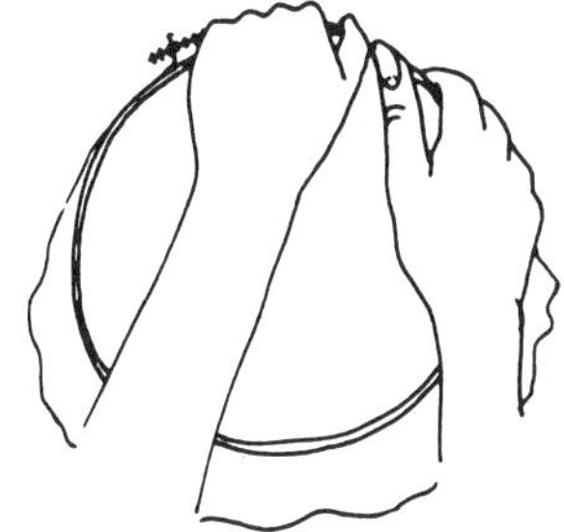

When the material is taut, push the upper ring down. To release the fabric do not unscrew the frame, but press thumbs down firmly into the fabric on the frame, at the same time lifting off the outer ring.

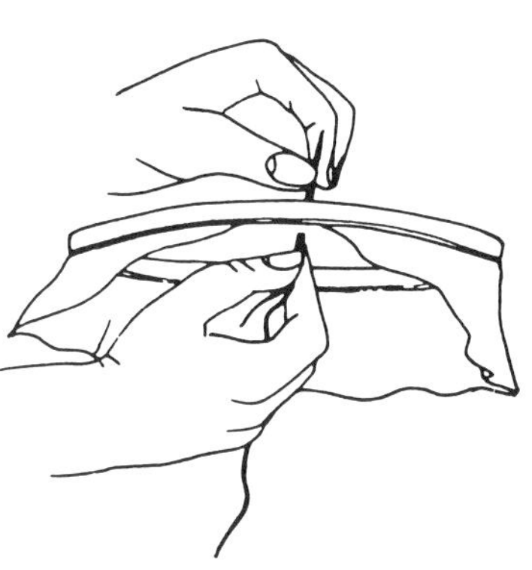

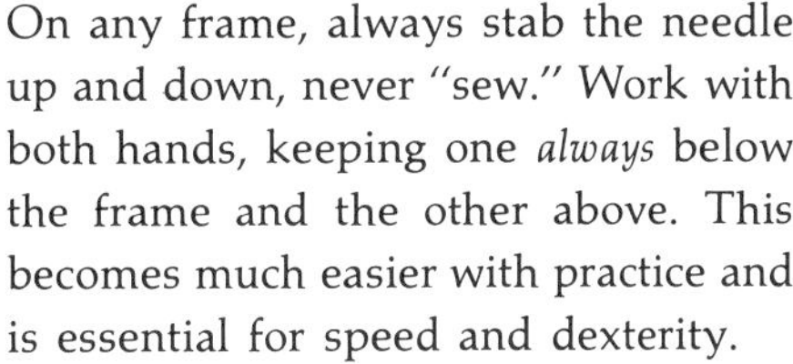

On any frame, always stab the needle up and down, never "sew." Work with both hands, keeping one *always* below the frame and the other above. This becomes much easier with practice and is essential for speed and dexterity.

The fourth choice is to use a square frame. This is delightful to work on since the material is always beautifully taut. The main disadvantage of a square frame is that it is awkward to move about. Secondly, it will only take material of the same width as itself. The length may be rolled around the rollers, but the width can only be that of the frame, 18 inches,

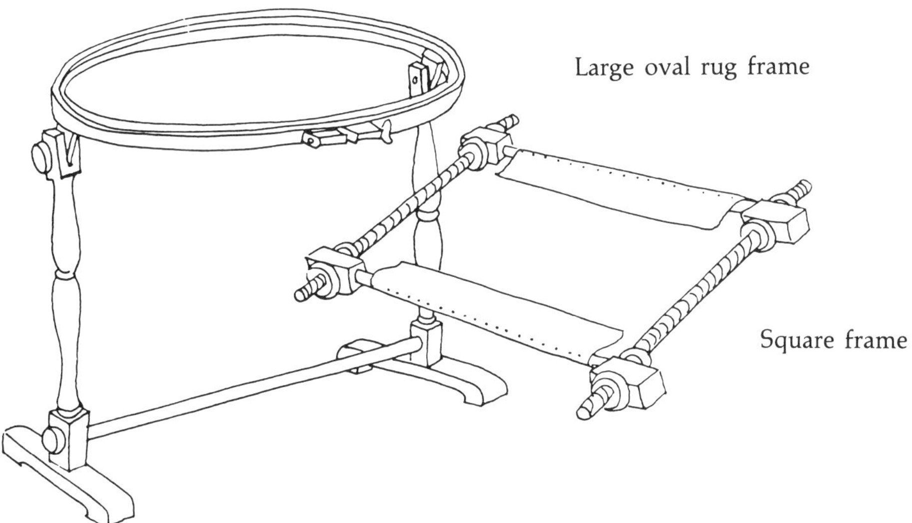

24 inches, or 36 inches (average frame sizes). So it is impossible to work a large bedspread on a square frame without having the frame made up to a special size. This is where a hoop frame, which is used just to stretch the area on which you are working, is especially useful.

It is perfectly possible, of course, to do crewel embroidery in your hand. The only drawback is that certain stitches are eliminated from your repertoire. You cannot lay long threads across a surface, and tie them down afterward, for instance, unless you have a firm foundation to work on. A great many people do extremely neat work without using a frame at all, but for the average person a good effect is far more easily gained with its help. When using either a table or floor ring frame and both hands, the speed, dexterity, and ease with which you work will surprise you. *The stitches for which a frame is essential are marked with an asterisk on the stitch diagrams—all others can be worked without it.*

MOUNTING WORK IN A SQUARE FRAME

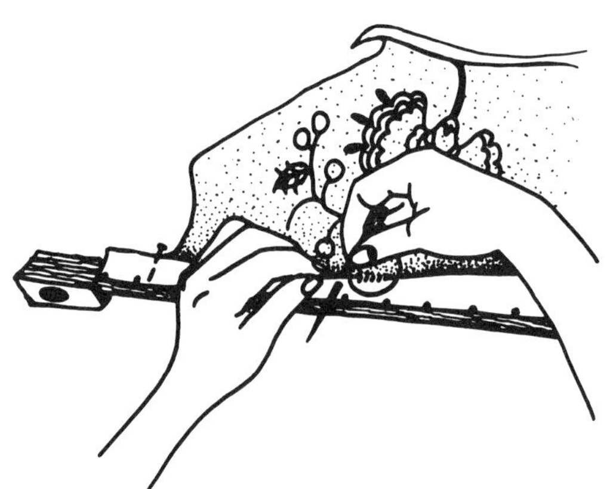

First stitch the fabric to the webbing of the square frame.

Then stretch tight, stitch webbing to either side and lace tightly with string as shown at right.

∗Many stitches can be worked either in the hand or in a frame. Some such as laid work, for instance, depend for their neatness on having the fabric stretched taut in the frame. Padded satin stitch and long and short stitch are others which are much easier when worked on a firm background. Therefore, those stitches for which a frame is essential are marked with an asterisk.∗

THE STITCHES

Since almost any stitches under the sun may be worked in silk or cotton, the important methods to describe here are those which are best suited for working with metal threads. The first and most versatile of these is couching. This can be done with so many variations and with such different effects it is scarcely recognizable as the same stitch. Therefore, the best way to become familiar with its different aspects is to experiment on a sampler. The wild arum on page 38 shows eight different methods which are described below.

*COUCHING

Couching may be worked as a plain outline, having the couching threads the same color as those underneath. Either one or two threads may be used in the needle and any number of threads may be couched down. Or two contrasting colors may be used, and the top stitches worked to form patterns. Couching may be used as a solid filling, working the threads back and forth or round in circles, or following the shape of the motif being filled. It may also be used as an open filling, called Random Couching, and is worked in any direction until the ground is evenly but lightly filled.

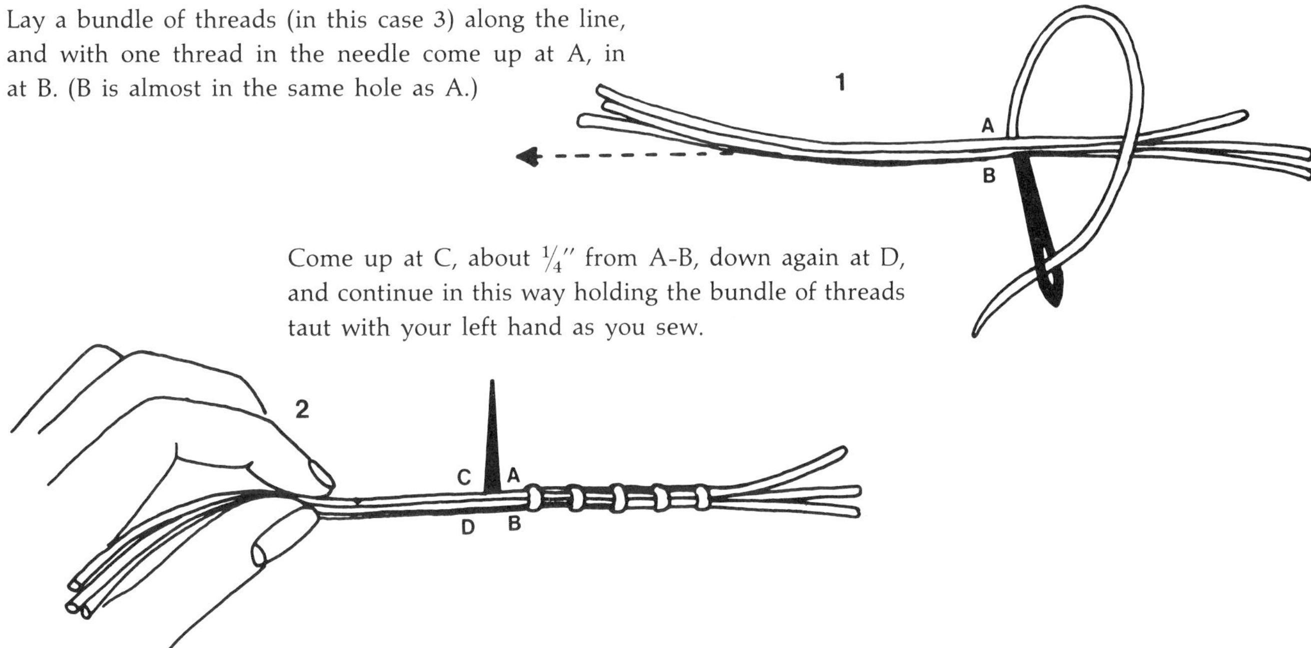

Lay a bundle of threads (in this case 3) along the line, and with one thread in the needle come up at A, in at B. (B is almost in the same hole as A.)

Come up at C, about ¼″ from A-B, down again at D, and continue in this way holding the bundle of threads taut with your left hand as you sew.

Wild arum lily, illustrating the stitches shown on the following pages (see key below)

- **A.** Random Couching
- **B.** Brick Pattern Couching
- **B.*** Couching with diagonal, straight and radiating line patterns
- **C.** Mille Fleur Pattern Couching
- **D.** Couching in a Circle
- **E.** Italian Shading, following the contours of the shape
- **F.** Burden Stitch, gold horizontal lines with silk stitching on top (see page 43)
- **G.** Couché Rentré
- **H.** Couched "plate" and braids (see page 21)

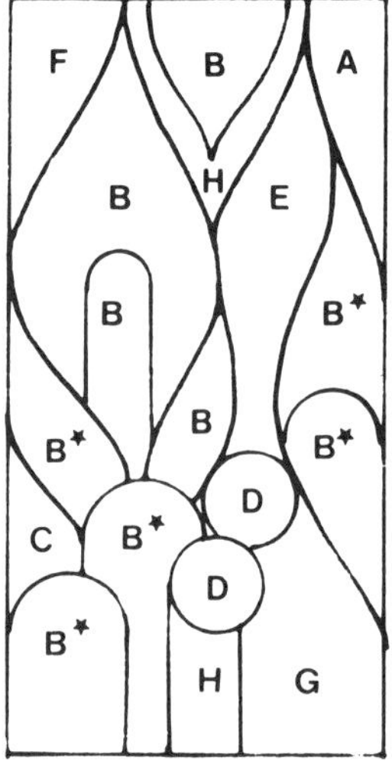

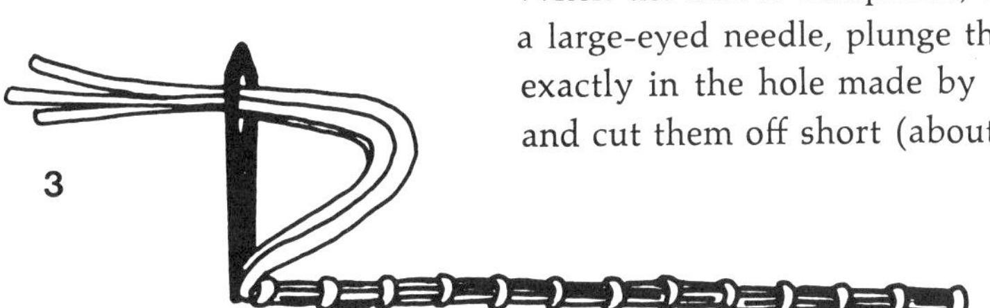

When the line is completed, thread the 3 threads into a large-eyed needle, plunge them through the material exactly in the hole made by the last couching stitch, and cut them off short (about 1/4") on reverse side.

Patterns may be made with the couching stitches (brick stitch shown). Always bring needle up on the outside, and go down close to the line already worked, so that no material shows between lines of couching. At the corners work couching stitch at the angle shown to make a sharp corner without having to plunge threads at the end of each line.

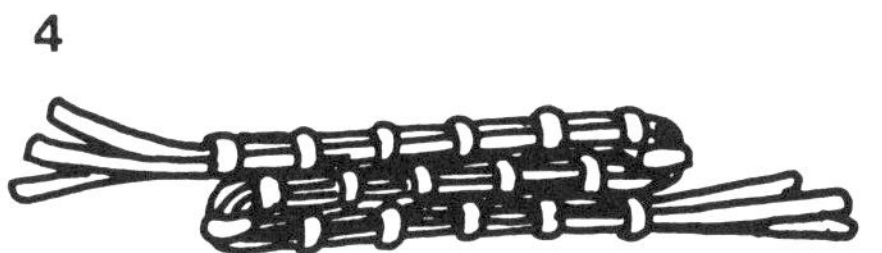

Random Couching (A) (Letters refer to sampler, page 38.)

Begin with the simplest form, random couching. Thread some waxed Maltese sewing silk (or any fine gold-colored buttonhole twist or mercerized sewing thread) into a #9 or #10 crewel needle. With this, sew down two threads of Japanese gold, following the directions for simple couching (see above), making a random meandering line as shown. Couching with *any* gold thread should always be done by sewing down a pair of threads rather than a single one. To sew individual threads would require too many couching stitches, diminishing the effect of the gold. Conversely, couching three threads at a time is apt to bunch them together, and it would be difficult to maintain a smooth flat line. Leave the ends of the couched gold threads lying on the surface until the whole area of stitching is complete.

Come up at A, and go down at B over the threads, sewing down the gold in a meandering line, with stitches at right angles and at regular intervals. When the line is complete, take the ends of gold through to the reverse side, as shown on the right.

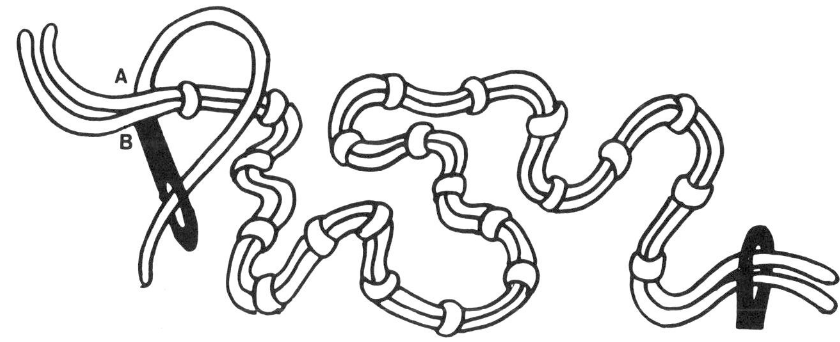

Then, using a large-eyed needle, take them through to the wrong side and cut them off. Leave the ends about $\frac{1}{4}$ inch long and let them hang loose on the back. The ends are too stiff and bulky to be secured on the reverse side, and they are so firmly stitched on the front that they will not work loose. If you take them through to the back *before* the area of needlework is completed, however, your stitches are apt to tangle with the ends on the back, making smooth stitching difficult.

Brick Pattern Couching (B and B*)

Fill the area with horizontal rows, turning the threads sharply at the end of each row by stitching each individual thread of the pair into its place separately, as shown. "Brick" the couching stitches to make a regular pattern by spacing them alternately as in the drawing. This method of couching is used to fill bandings, borders, and larger shapes solidly. If the brick pattern is done with matching gold-colored thread, the couching stitches become almost invisible, giving the effect of a solid gold fabric laid down on the surface.

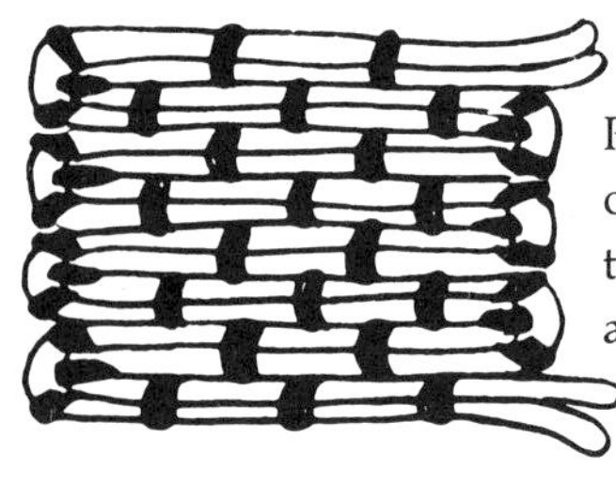

Place the lines of gold close side by side, but not so tightly packed that they overlap one another. As you turn at the end of each line, hold the corners out square by placing two stitches on the outer gold thread, one on the inner. Then continue along the line, alternating the couching stitches to form a brick pattern.

Mille Fleur Pattern Couching (C)

Next, try making patterns other than the brick, such as the "mille fleur," using a contrasting color thread. You may find it helpful to mark out the material with lines at regular intervals to guide you as you work down, row by row.

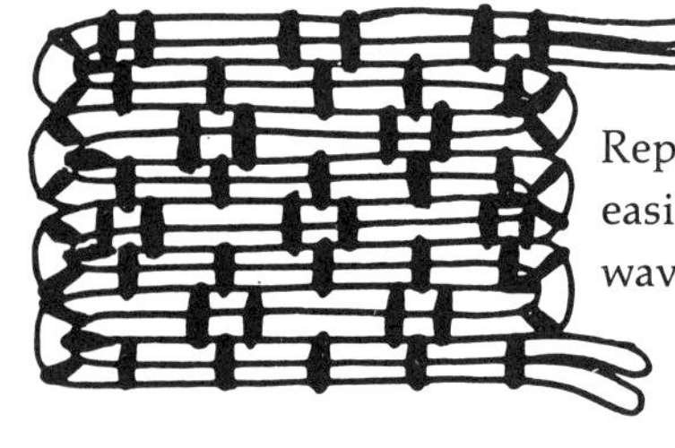

Repeat B, but arrange the stitches to form the grouping shown here. Other patterns can easily be made, as you hold down each row with couching stitches, such as diagonal or wavy lines, or chevron patterns.

Couching in a Circle (D)

Then try couching to fill a circle. With a pencil, lightly draw regularly spaced lines radiating out from the center of the circle, and use these as a guide for your couching stitches. Fold in half one length of gold thread to be used for the couching and start by sewing down the loop end of this doubled thread in the center of the circle. Work round and round in widening rings, sewing down the two gold strands together, and placing a couching stitch on each pencil line. Make sure no material shows between the rows of couching, yet do not crowd the rows so closely that they overlap one another. To end off with a smooth outline at the edge of the circle, plunge one gold thread through the fabric slightly ahead of the other.

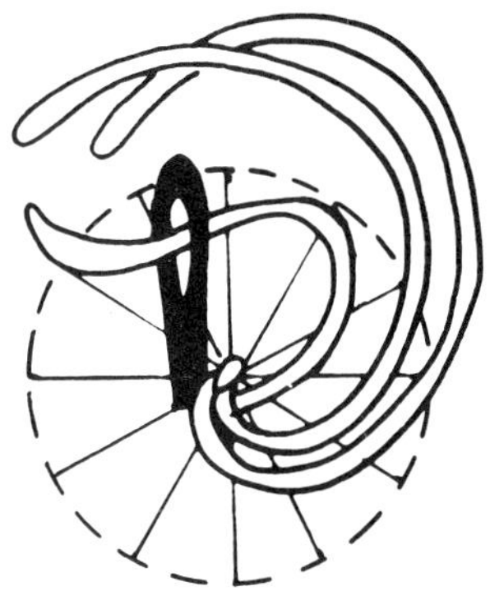

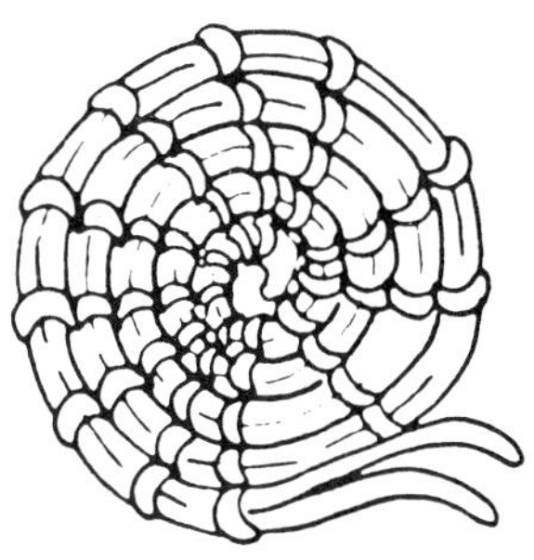

Showing the beginning, and the finished effect

Couching to Fill a Shape (B*)

Contrary to a circle, a shape like this is best started at the edge, working round and round to the center, "bricking" the stitches as shown. The dotted lines are pencilled on the fabric as a guide for the couching stitches. At each corner sew over each gold thread separately on the angle of the dotted line (as shown below).

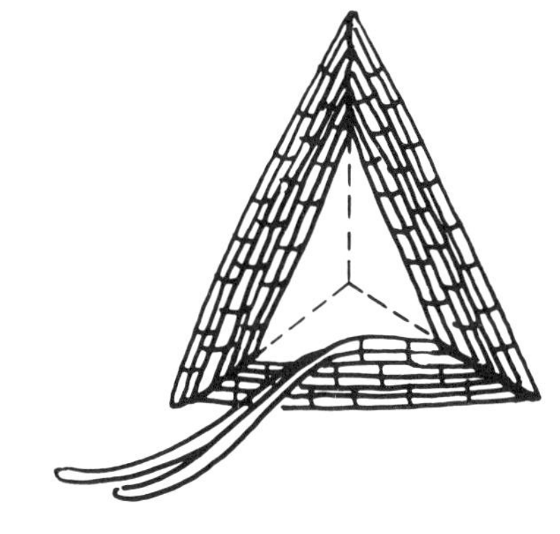

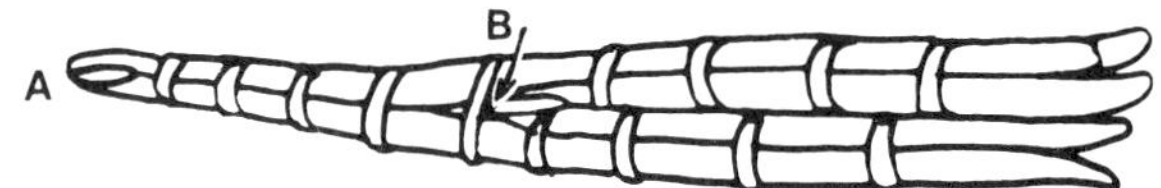

Filling a Long Narrow Shape

When the shape to be filled is very thin and tapering, take only *one* of the pair of gold threads to the outer limit of the narrow shape (at A) and sew it down with a double stitch for firmness at this point. Then double it on itself working it back to meet the second thread (at B). Turn *this* thread back sharply, stitching it with a double stitch, and continue them both together, as the shape widens, making a smooth flowing line as shown.

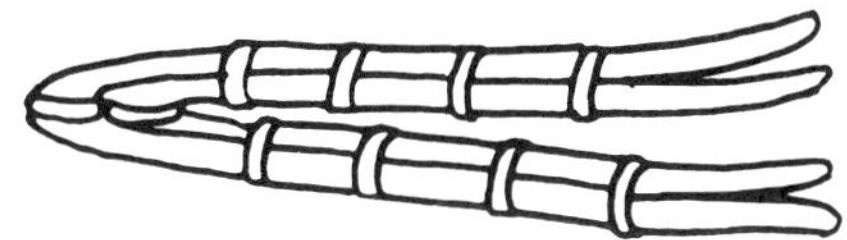

Couching a Sharp Pointed Corner

Showing each gold thread sewn down separately at the point

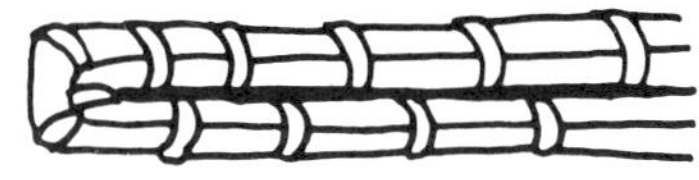

Couching a Square Corner

*ITALIAN SHADING (E)

Finally, you are ready to try the most sophisticated form of couching, which is known as Italian shading. This can be done in two ways. The first is to lay your gold thread in the contours of the shape, using the couching stitches for shading. You can shade by varying both the colors and density of the tiny stitches as you take them over your gold thread (as shown in the wild arum at E).

The second technique is to lay your gold threads in row upon row of straight lines touching one another, creating a design or pattern with the couching stitches as you go along. (E on your sampler.) In this technique the gold becomes merely a solid background surface, and the design is created by the variation of tiny couching stitches that are used to hold the gold thread flat. The spacing or closeness of these stitches allows the gold to shimmer through occasionally, giving a mosaic effect. The best way to work is to have several needles threaded, each with its own color, so that you can use them as you reach each area to be worked in that shade, as shown below. (Note: It is not necessary to wax your couching thread for Italian shading; see page 45.)

Shading, following the contours of a shape. The gold threads have been completely covered with close couching stitches inside the lily to give a dark shadow effect. The couching stitches are then spaced gradually wider apart and the colors lightened towards the outer edge of the shape. This couching is done line by line, just like B.

Italian shading, building up the pattern as you go along, line by line, each needle threaded with the color required for that area

*BURDEN STITCH (F)

A variation of Italian shading is burden stitch. This stitch consists of regularly spaced threads laid horizontally across the shape, held flat with a brick work of vertical stitches on top. Though the stitch is frequently worked entirely with wool in crewel embroidery, it can be most effective with the horizontal stitches underneath in gold and vertical ones on top in silk. When worked in this way it really resembles Italian shading worked openly instead of solidly. First couch down the horizontal rows of gold thread, using a matching waxed silk thread, so that the stitches are invisible. The spacing between each row depends on the background fabric, and how fine or bold you want the finished result to be. Then work the vertical stitches in silk to form a brick pattern on top. This top stitching may be so close that the gold just gleams through, or could be of such gossamer fineness that the silk or cotton only forms a light network over the surface of the bold metal threads. (See page 95.)

*COUCHÉ RENTRÉ (G)

When discussing intriguing variations of couching, one cannot ignore the medieval method of couching called couché rentré. This magnificently effective stitchery is a means of completely covering the background linen with gold threads, and has the effect of flame stitch or bargello stitchery worked in solid gold. It can be done on canvas or linen and you may ask why not sew with regular brick stitch to get the same effect?

The stitching is shown on a mesh background to suggest the open weave linen necessary for couché rentré. The fabric must be stretched firmly in a frame and a strong waxed double silk or cotton thread should be used to couch the pairs of gold threads. Come up at A, go over the gold threads and return to A again, going down in the exact same hole. Pull sharply, so that the gold thread jumps right through the fabric, and continue to repeat the procedure for the next stitch. Work in straight lines, cutting the threads and "plunging" them (see page 45) at the end of each line. This makes an easier and neater edge than turning them at the end of each line, on the open weave linen.

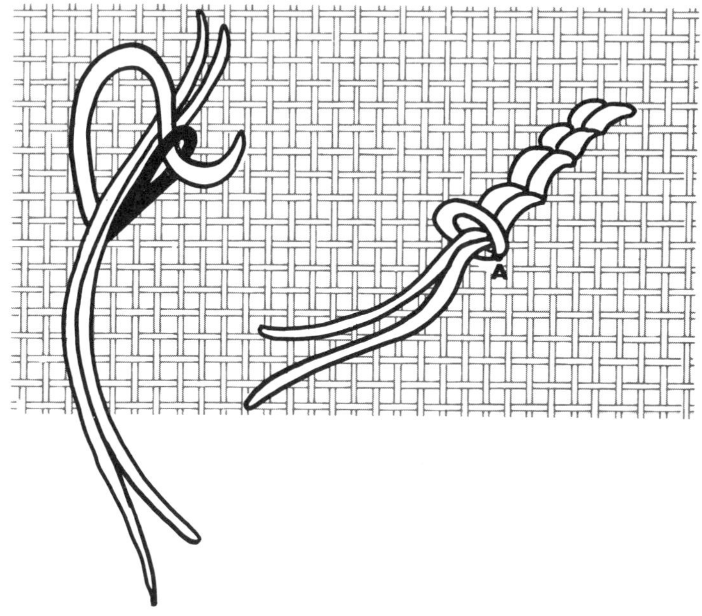

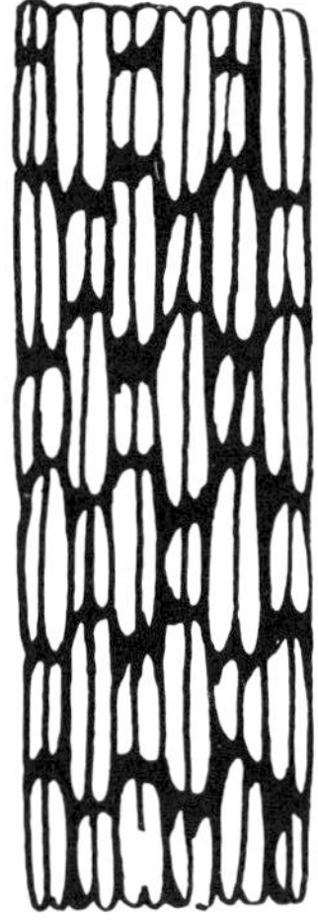
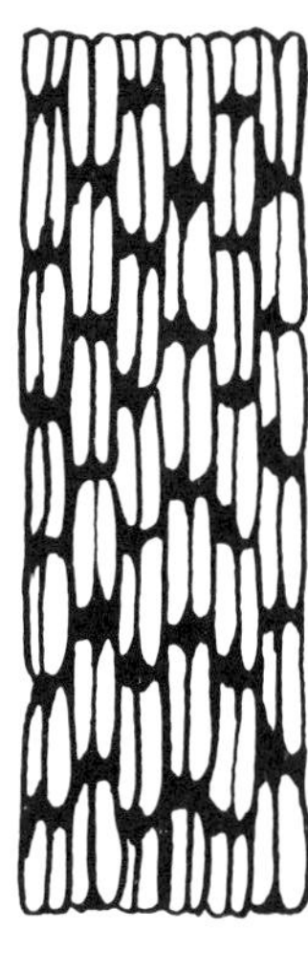
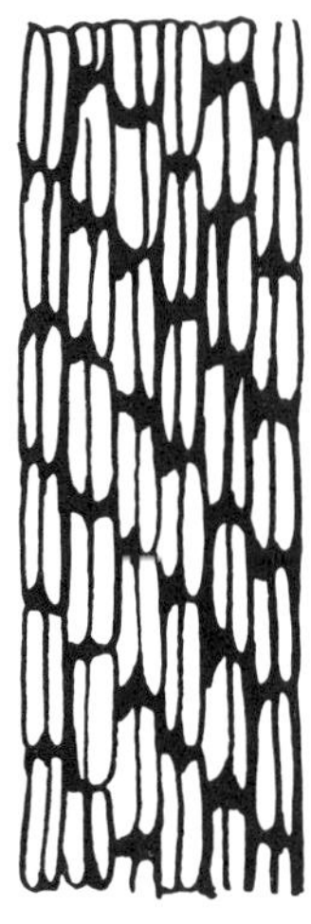

By varying the relative positions of the couching stitches, all kinds of patterns can be made, as shown here.

The answer is that even the most pliable Lurex is sometimes a difficult thread to use for large background areas when you have to stitch right through the fabric. Small lengths of thread would have to be used or they would tear as they pass through it, and of course Japanese gold would be out of the question, as it would be much too fragile. Therefore, couché rentré with its surface couching, which only *appears* to be stitched right through, is an excellent solution.

*COUCHING CORDS

Couching gold, silk, or wool cords can be done invisibly so that the cord appears to be lying on the surface without stitches to attach it. Braids are a little more difficult, and usually have to be sewn with minute stitches first on one side, then on the other to hold them invisibly.

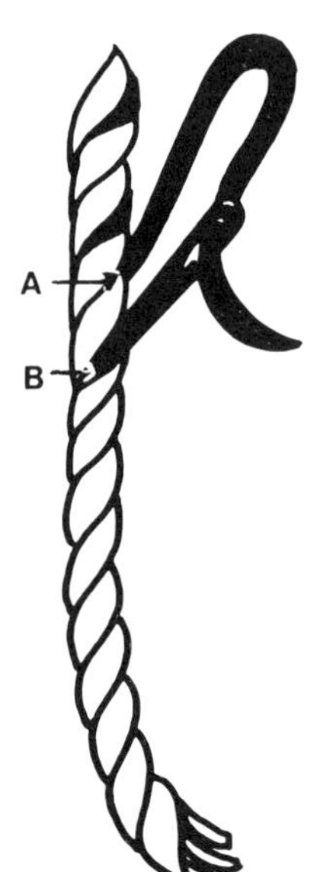

Come up at A, on the outside of the cord but close to it. Go down at B right in the center of the cord, between the twists. This makes a small slanting stitch, which, when pulled firmly, lies parallel with the twists and disappears completely. Place the stitches about two or three twists apart. It is not necessary to stitch every one.

Shows a wide braid, sewn with small, almost invisible stitches on either side

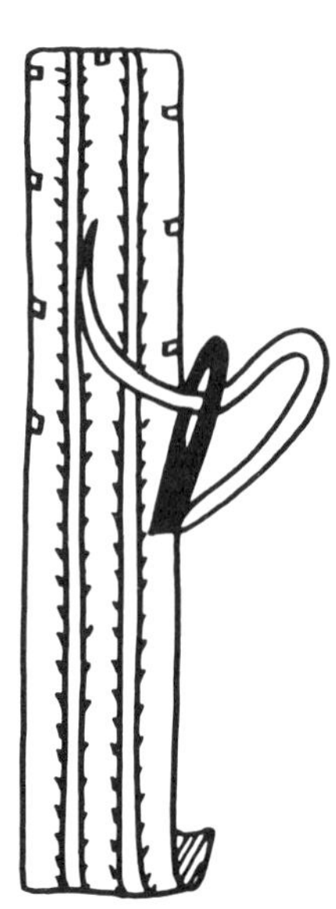

RAISED GOLD OVER STRING/Raised Outlines

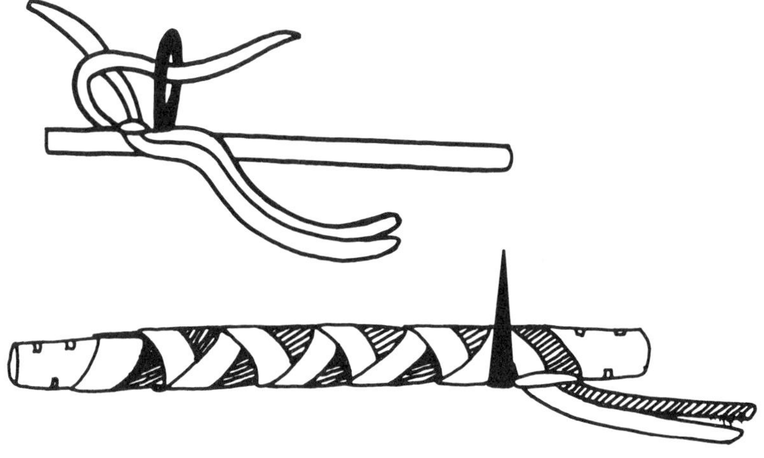

1. Sew two threads of gold (or one of silk and one of gold) over a line of string which has been stitched to the fabric. Take a double stitch over the gold, close to and parallel with the string.

2. Then fold the gold over the string and repeat this double stitch on the other side. "Plunge" the ends of gold through the material when the line is complete.

PLUNGING

To "plunge" heavy cords or braids you may need to pierce a hole in the material with a stiletto (see page 28) or a large needle. Then you can easily take the ends of the thread through this hole to the wrong side. Ease them through, one by one, to avoid damaging them, and cut them off, leaving the ends to hang loose, about $\frac{1}{4}$ inch long.

Shows a heavy cord being plunged by taking the needle into the fabric, and then threading it. Push the ends of cord only a little way through the eye, so that the thread will not be too heavy to pull through. If necessary, open a hole in the fabric with the closed ends of sharp pointed scissors, or a stiletto, so that the cord will slip through more easily.

Things to remember about couching:

1. Always wax your silk or cotton couching thread to protect it and prevent the metal from cutting it. One exception is Italian shading, where the close stitches provide such strong protection that waxing is unnecessary.

Further, the waxing tends to darken the thread, which would spoil the vibrant color necessary for Italian shading.

2. Keep couching stitches at right angles to the gold threads, and space them so that the gold is held firm; yet not so closely covered with stitching that it cannot gleam through.
3. Gauge the width and tension of each couching stitch. If the stitches are too narrow they tend to pucker the two threads on top of each other, forming a wasp waist at each stitch. Alternatively, if the stitches are too wide the gold threads will move about.
4. Make all corners and points sharp and slightly exaggerated to give a crisp, clear-cut effect.
5. Handle the Japanese gold as little as possible. Should it separate, twist it back and hold it in place so that the silk core is covered as you sew it down.
6. "Plunge" the gold with a very large needle to avoid tearing the threads as you take them through to the wrong side. Use a stiletto to open a hole in the background fabric before plunging heavy cords or braids.

PADDING

Couching on a padded surface achieves completely different effects. The chariot riders (opposite) shows this both in the process of work and as a finished design. First try padding with string. Fill the area to be raised with horizontal rows of string sewn down approximately $\frac{1}{4}$ inch apart. Using a fine thread, waxed for strength, sew down each length of string with small stitches taken first on one side and then on the other. To make clear edges, carefully cut the string at the end of each line with a razor blade as soon as it has been stitched in place. Take great care not to slit through the background material; cut *only* the string! Now take a pair of gold threads and couch them over the string at right angles to it.

By alternating the positions of the couching stitches you can make patterns as shown in the diagram, catching down the gold after it has passed over one line of string, then over two, then over one again to form regular repeat patterns.

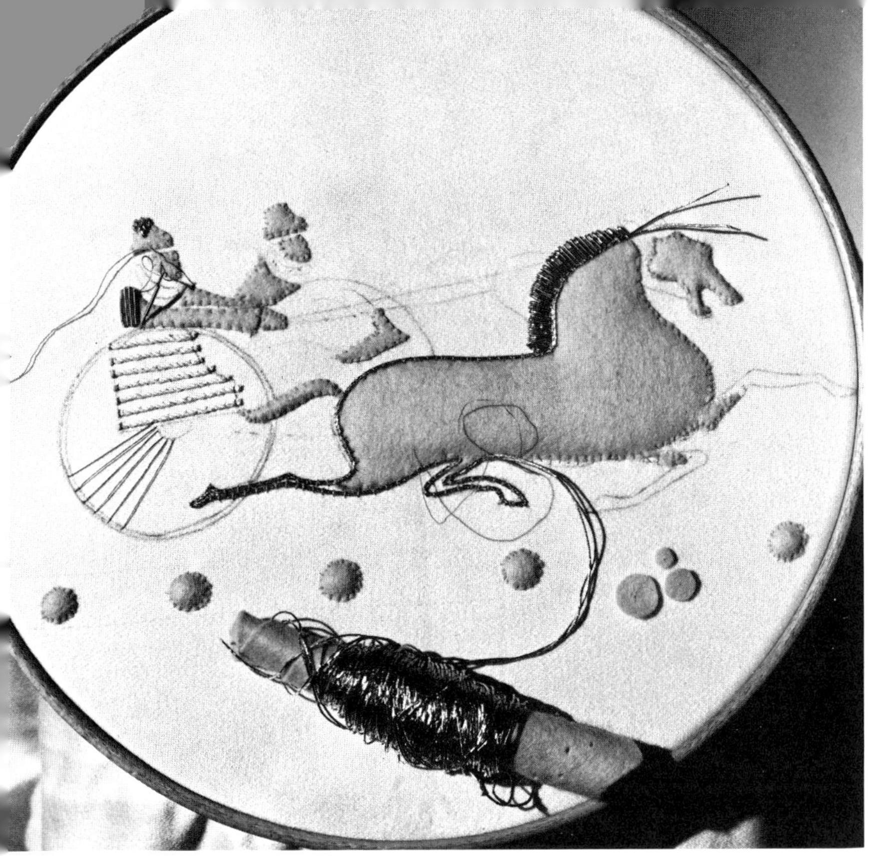

The Chariot Riders. Adapted from a Chinese clay tablet 102 B.C. *Worked by the author*

ABOVE

Chariot shows parallel lines of string stitched down horizontally. Horse and riders have been padded with three layers of felt. On lower border right hand circle shows three sizes of felt ready to be stitched down, one on top of the other.

BELOW

The completed design. Chariot: Japanese gold couched vertically over string; riders and mane: rough and smooth bullion; hats: check bullion in small chips; horse: couched Japanese gold. Lower border: couched Japanese gold, raised only at intervals over felt circles

PADDING WITH STRING

Sewing down evenly spaced rows of string.

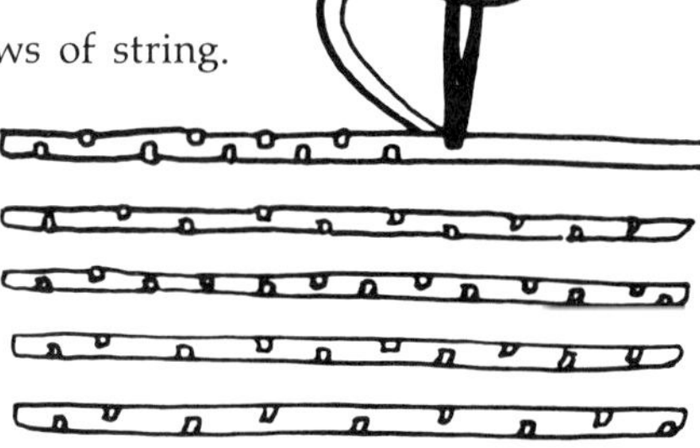

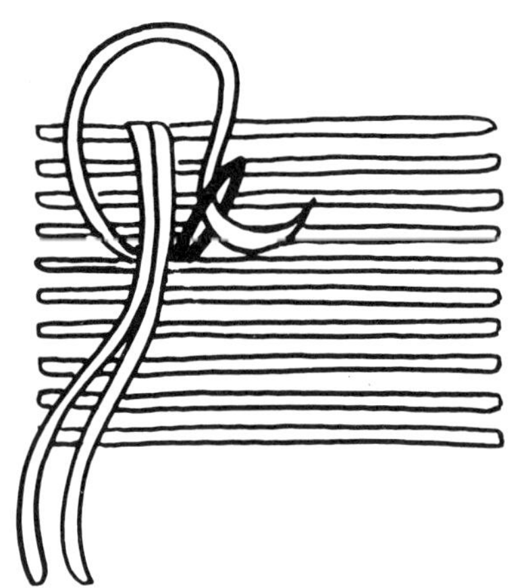

Sew down a pair of gold threads (or one of gold and one of silk) at the top of the rows of string. (Take each couching stitch twice for firmness). Go over four threads of string, and catch down the gold between the rows, again taking a double stitch.

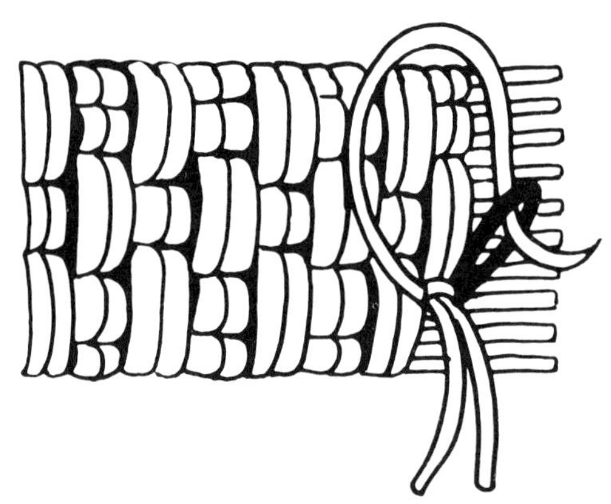

Next, go over two threads, then over four, then over two again as shown. Work two identical lines in this pattern, side by side. Then work two more lines alternating the pattern (going over four threads next to the two taken on the previous row, and two next to the four, etc.). This will form a brick pattern as shown. Any number of patterns can be worked out by simply couching the threads over different numbers of rows of string.

PADDING WITH FELT

To pad with felt, draw an oval or circle on your sampler and cut a piece of yellow felt to fit it exactly. Then cut four more pieces, each one smaller than the previous one, so that you have a stack of five layers of felt each decreasing in size. Starting with the smallest first, sew this in the center of your shape, securing it all around with tiny stitches at right angles to the edge. Keep these stitches close together to prevent the edges from puckering. Repeat, sewing down successively larger layers, to build up a smooth raised surface which is higher in the center. Next draw your couching lines on the padded oval or circle (i.e., a radiating sunburst or spiraling effect). However, for a simple brick pattern there is no need to draw guide lines as the stitches themselves will control your spacing. Now couch the gold thread closely over the felt following the instructions on page 41 for couching in a circle.

Sewing down three layers of felt

Start by sewing the smallest circle of felt in the center of the shape. Come up outside the shape, and go down into the felt, making small stitches at right angles to the edge.

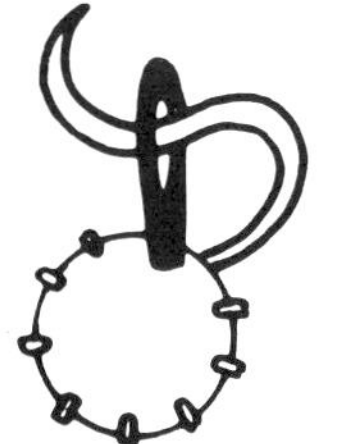

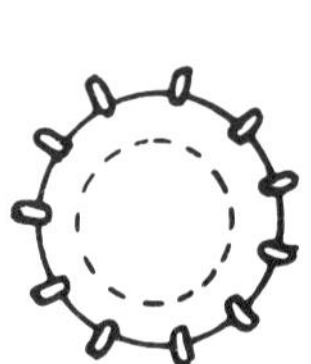

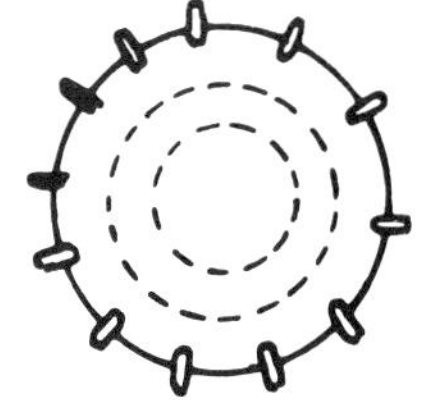

Sew the next layer on top. Finally, sew the largest top layer down.

Starting in the center, couch the gold threads round and round, stitching right through the felt.

Padded Italian Shading

Felt padding may also be used in combination with Italian shading, either following the contours or by covering the area with close horizontal lines. Here the padded felt circles were sewn down at intervals. Then couched lines of gold were taken right across from side to side. At the edges of each circle take the couching stitches close together to outline the shape. Cover the whole area by couching one line after the other right across the shape, going over both raised and flat areas with continuous lines. (See base of chariot riders, page 47.)

BULLION

The bullion threads described on page 24 may also be worked over a padding of string or felt.

Prepare a handy board for cutting the bullion by gluing a piece of felt to a square of cardboard. The board is necessary because if cut on any smooth or shiny surface the little chips of bullion fly in a thousand directions and are lost. The felt has a kind of magnetic quality for them. To determine the length of the first piece, hold the bullion across the area to be covered and kink it gently with your scissors. Bring it back to the

Silk on fine wool background, sails padded with felt. *Designed by the author, worked by Mrs. Hampton Lynch*

Pomegranate tree showing different methods of padding with felt and string; to obtain crisp edges, small leaves are sewn over cardboard of postcard thickness. *Worked by Mary Haddon, designed by the author*

board and cut it right through, using this as your guide for the length of the next pieces. Do not cut bullion pieces more than $\frac{1}{2}$ inch long or they will crack as you sew them down. However, if they are cut too short they will not cover the padding. Getting them just the right length is the whole skill in this technique.

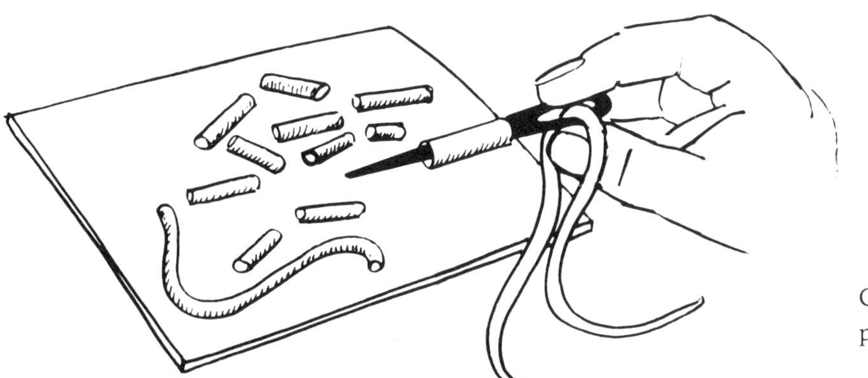

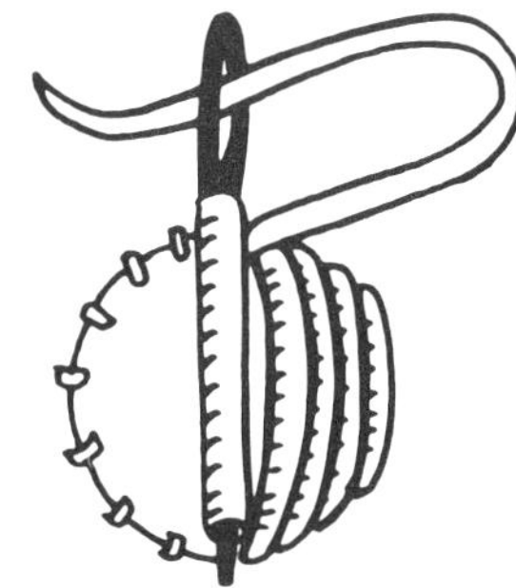

Cutting bullion thread on a board, and preparing to sew it down like a bead

Sewing down small chips of bullion to cover the padded felt, with stitches taken in different directions like seeding

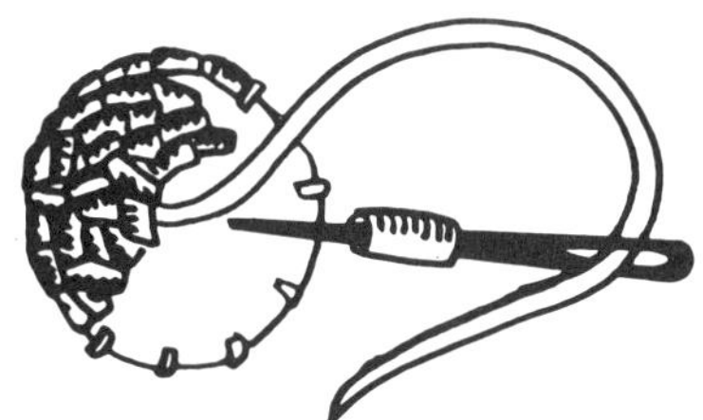

Large areas should be filled with patterns (such as brick or chevron) formed from short pieces of bullion, completely covering the padded felt area. The check or frisé bullion generally looks best when it is cut into tiny chips and sewn down in all different directions to cover the felt completely. This is more time-consuming but a great deal easier than making the smooth rows with the other types of bullion.

All the foregoing has purposely been limited to strictly traditional techniques. They are important to know since, just as in classical ballet where the disciplines of traditional steps are the foundations of modern dance, the knowledge will improve your ability when you take off on free contemporary experiments. Once you have tried the traditional methods there is no reason why you could not take the bullion or pearl purl and couch them down with other threads as in the milkweed pod on page 52. Or incorporate long strips of bullion sewn down flat with gold clock wheels, or semi-precious stones—or fake ones! Or you could combine

Milkweed pod in gold couching with silk thread. *Designed and worked by Dorothy Hickey*

the silk and gold threads with appliqué, with crewel wool stitchery, or with stump work, experimenting with the stitches in any way you please.

BLOCKING AND CLEANING

Plain silk embroidery can be blocked just like crewel embroidery, but face downward, as a flat smooth finish is generally desired. Before blocking, test the color of the embroidery thread and the background fabric to make sure they are colorfast. Most silk and cotton threads are boilfast, but it's certainly better to be safe than sorry!

Since most gold and silver embroidery has to be done on a frame it will probably need little blocking. If it should have been rolled, or the background material folded, press it face down into thick layers of white Turkish toweling, covered with a smooth hand towel, or even a soft pillow slip. Use a warm iron and press firmly, allowing the plunged ends of couching, which are often bunched together on the wrong side, to remain

Various bullion threads worked flat and over string. *Designed and worked by Barbara Dawson*

free. Do not press them down flat; they may leave an unwanted impression on the front of the material.

Cleaning could be a problem when water tarnishes the gold. It is fortunate that Lurex threads are completely washable. In the sixteenth century, metal threads were burnished by being rubbed with red velvet to restore their luster, but all through the ages the best cleaning agent has been white bread, crumbled up and rubbed over the surface. French chalk, that fine powdered talc-like substance, has also been a mainstay. Let it lie thickly on top of the embroidery for as long as possible (overnight or longer), then bang and shake the needlework to remove all traces of powder and, hopefully, the dirt!

BLOCKING

To block the finished work, first soak the embroidery in cold water, and lay it, dripping wet, on a board or old table which has been first covered with a sheet. If the embroidery is raised, lay it out right side uppermost; if it is flat and a smooth finished result is needed, put it right side down. Then, with carpet tacks, nail down the four corners first, measuring the opposite sides to see that they are even and making sure the corners are true right angles. You may have to pull the material out with pliers to make sure it is really taut. Then nail down four more tacks, one in the center of each side, and then eight more in the spaces between. Continue round and round, adding in this way more tacks until they are about 1/4 inch apart. Allow the fabric to dry. When it is thoroughly dry, take it up, and if it is not being mounted immediately, roll it round a cardboard tube with the embroidery outward (so that the stitches are not crushed against one another).

Tack down the design, placing one carpet tack in each corner first.

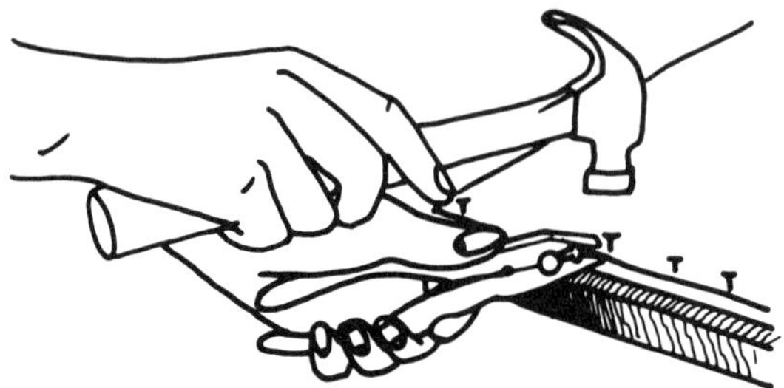

Tack the fabric all around, pulling it out flat with pliers so that it is really taut.

STUMP WORK

Court gown at the wedding of the Prince of Orange to the daughter of George II:

Embroidered with chenille, the pattern a large stone vase filled with ramping flowers, that spread over a breadth of the petticoat from the bottom to the top; between each vase was a pattern of gold shells and foliage, embossed, and most heavily rich, the gown was white satin, embroidered also with chenille mixed with gold ornaments, no vases on the sleeve, but two or three on the tail!

Side panel from a stump work box shown on page 70, using stitches such as ceylon and trellis (see pages 85 and 84). *Victoria and Albert Museum*

CURIOUSER and curiouser!" said Alice, following the twisting path of the White Rabbit. This might be the perfect way to describe the "raised" or "embossed" work of the seventeenth and eighteenth centuries, which later became known, strangely enough, as "stump work."

The raised work done in England at this time, where it seemed to be particularly fashionable, consisted mostly of mirror frames, boxes with compartments for toilet and writing articles, with perhaps even a secret drawer, and pictures and small bags. These were done in the very finest of stitches, with tremendous virtuosity and finesse, often by young girls who had suddenly discovered the delight of stitching these charming little motifs in relief on white satin.

The designs were often similar, nearly always consisting of two central figures on either side of a fountain, the surrounding garden being a space-filling of flowers, fruits, plants, and animals, all happily oblivious of scale. Into these charming formalized gardens went ladies and gentlemen all looking remarkably alike with their ruffs and bodices, brocaded skirts and pantaloons, whether they were supposed to represent James I and his Queen, Susannah and the Elders, the Five Senses, or even the Four Continents.

Why this raised embroidery should suddenly have become all the rage and why it should have been called "stump work" are mysteries fascinating to explore.

Two explanations for the name are generally given. One is that, because the raised effect was sometimes obtained by covering little boxwood molds with stitching, the technique came to be called "embroidery on the stump." Or, perhaps because patterns printed on satin were available to the embroideress for the first time, "embroidery on the stamp" eventually became "stump work." Neither of these explanations seems totally satisfactory, however. For the curious, a third is worthy of some sleuth work. *Estompé* is the French word for embossed. In 1678 the phrase stump drawing—directly derived from *estompé*—was introduced into the Oxford

Dictionary for the first time. Stump drawing was a form of shaded pencil sketching which gave to the flat picture the effect of high relief. Pencil-shaped cylinders of paper, soft leather, or India rubber, called stumps, were used to rub down hard pencil lines and produce soft rounded effects. It seems logical to suppose, or at any rate interesting to conjecture, that a new and fashionable word describing drawing in relief might also have been borrowed to describe embossed embroidery. It was only after this date, in the eighteenth century, that raised or embossed needlework became generally known as "stump work."

By the eighteenth century, raised embroidery with gold threads,

Scenes from the Biblical story of David in typical 17th-century style. *Victoria and Albert Museum*

The Lord Chancellor's Purse, in a design dating back to the 17th century. *Crown Copyright*

pearls, and jewels had become a tradition in France, where almost every girl seemed to have been born with a needle in her hand. As early as the twelfth century, French cathedrals and churches were so numerous and their contents so rich that a popular contemporary phrase was "happy as God in France." The lavish splendor of the court of Le Roi Soleil had not subsided when Louis XV took his place, and embroidery was used to enrich everything: no longer was it restricted to ecclesiastical use. In fact, Louis XV himself claimed that he could do better embroidery than anyone else in his entire kingdom!

This description by the Marquise de Créqui of the dress of one of the ladies of Louis' court shows to what lengths (or rather, heights!) raised work was sometimes taken. "The dress was of rich red velvet. The folds of the ample skirt were held in position by brooches of Dresden china made in the semblance of butterflies. On a front panel of the dress was embroidered a design showing an orchestra complete with musical instruments. *The latter were worked in relief* and the musicians embroidered on cloth of silver were arranged in six rows. Within the skirt was a hoop of nearly six yards in circumference."

English ladies, intrigued by a technique so new to them, developed a completely original approach in design and concept, in the same way as their Colonial cousins, who were transplanting the English crewelwork into their own American idiom at almost the same time.

Although the designs and techniques of English stump work seem unique, there are several logical reasons for its development apart from its continental influence. Gardens, samplers, and pattern books, for instance, all played their part in inspiring the designs, while in stitchery the influence may have come from raised embroidered book bindings, canvas work appliquéd to velvet, and needlepoint lace, with its variety of stitches worked free from the background fabric.

First of all, the fascination of the embroideress for the garden setting is better understood if we realize that in the seventeenth century everything was relatively new to the young girl, whose preoccupation was translating this excitement into silken stitches on satin. Until then, gardens had been cultivated exclusively at monasteries or castles, and even when they became part of the surroundings of the manor house, they were reserved at first for herbs and vegetables.

Because "sallads" were so popular, "longwort, liverwort and purslane" were grown together with yarrow, sorrel, and borage, which caused Parkinson, in 1629, to suggest that the kitchen garden be removed from the front of the house, "for the many different scents which arrise from the herbes such as cabbages, onions, etc., are scarce well pleasing to perfume the lodgings of any house." However, "sallets," as they were also called, included the candied petals of roses, violets, cowslips, and strawberry leaves, and it is easy to see how these favorites would take their place alongside such sophisticated flowers as the opium poppy from the Middle East, the sunflower from Mexico, potato and tobacco plants from the New World, and the tulip, newly arrived from Istanbul via Holland. The Elizabethan flower gardens, with their formal borders and hedges of musk, lavender, and rosemary, their new flowers—hyacinths, pinks, marigolds, and iris—all blending their fragrances around a central fountain and pool "whose shaking crystal was a perfect mirror for all its other beauties," could rightly inspire Sir William Cecil to say: "For if delight may provoke men's labour, what greater delight is there than to behold the earth apparelled with plants, as with a robe of imbroidered works, set with orient pearles and garnished with great diversitie of rare and costly jewels."

And so, with great "diversitie," the stump-work garden would be planned, peopled with figures whose faces were sometimes raised with sculptured wooden molds under the silken stitching, whose stomachers or bodices, padded with wool or horsehair, often surmounted skirts in brilliant petit point. These were embroidered separately, then gathered or pleated, and attached only at the waist, so that the skirt could be lifted to disclose a froth of lace petticoats and perhaps a pair of golden shoes. Butterflies, flitting among the flowers, would have two sets of wings—one embroidered flat on the satin background and the other free-standing in lacy buttonhole

A garden scene from Petrus Crescentius, *Opus Ruralium Commodarum. British Museum*

Left and right side of an 18th-century mirror frame

stitches. Peapods that could be raised to show the tiny seed pearl peas within, caterpillars in fluffy chenille threads, and of course the fountain in gold or silver bullion, were all primly surrounded by the rainbow-hued flowers.

The young lady who loved stump work must necessarily have learned the basic stitches on her sampler when she was a child—cross stitch, then possibly tent stitch, Florentine and rococo stitches, or even plaited braid or chain stitch in gold thread on the linen. She might have interspersed these with panels of cut and drawn work, or made a separate record of those in a white work sampler.

Indeed, it was the custom to teach girls their alphabet at the same time as needlework. As early as the seventeenth century, the importance of this exercise in their education and the extreme youth of the students are shown by this extract from a letter written by the Countess of Traquair. Practically penniless and in exile in Paris, she nonetheless struggled to provide her daughter, Lady Anne Maxwell, with the "necessarys." These were masters ". . . of whom she has 4, a dancing master, a singing master, a harpsicall master and a French master. For since perhaps she may never have wherwithall to portion her, she stands more in need of good qualitys, so that I am willing to squeeze it out, even out of necessarys to myselfe, thinking her education preferable to my wants. . . . But between all these her day is pretty well employd; for she has her English reading, and her sampler, and has done already the 24* letters twice over, both sides alike, and all her masters are satisfyd with her." All this, and Lady Anne not yet five years old!

Yet there are no samplers entirely worked in raised embroidery remaining to us today. This is probably because the stump work was almost a sampler itself: a progression from the basic stitches to a chef d'oeuvre which would incorporate the more complex techniques from many types of embroidery. It was almost as though the young lady, carefully schooled from her early years, would graduate with a beautifully worked cabinet or mirror frame which would show all her skill in one magnificent piece.

One part of this grand project with which she did not have to struggle was drawing her own design. Numerous herbals, gardening books, and bestiaries, even designs on separate sheets, were available to the

*I and J and U and V were interchangeable in early alphabets.

Elizabethan embroiderer for the first time, to arrange as she liked. Many of the plates from the few rare books which have survived are pricked for copying.

> Here followeth certaine Patternes of Cut-workes newly invented and never published before. Also sundry sorts of spots as Flowers, Birdes and Fishes, etc., and will fitly serve to be wrought some with gould some with silke, some with crewell in coullers, or otherwise at your pleasure. (London, printed in Shoe Lane at the Sign of the Faulcon, by Richard Shorleyker.)

> A catalogue of Plates, and pictures that are printed and sold by Peter Stent dwelling at the sign of the white Horfe in Gilt Spur Street betwixt Newgate and Py Corner. (1662)

Just as gardens, samplers, and pattern books played their part in forming the design for stump work, so three styles of needlework originating in the sixteenth century all contributed to the development of its stitchery.

The first was the fashion for stitched book bindings. One of the earliest known embroidered books was given as a New Year's gift to Queen Elizabeth in 1583. It was described as "a large Byble in Englysshe covered with crymson vellat alover embrodered with venys gold and seade perle."* Later book bindings embroidered in silk on satin were found to wear much longer if seed pearls and raised gold were combined with the flat stitching. In many cases, the gold used was "purl" or "bullion," a silver gilt wire coil, which the embroideress would cut into short lengths and sew down like a bead, threading the needle through the center of the coiled tube (see page 49).

This raised effect gave the book covers a tremendous richness, and several that have been left to us today are in perfect condition because they in turn were enclosed in embroidered bags to protect them. The gold bullion embroidery worked on book bindings also was used for stump work. Fortunately, like the books, a very few embroidered cabinets were preserved in specially made cases, which enables us to see even today the brilliant sparkle of the gold thread, instead of a tarnished and lusterless gray.

A second influence, which inadvertently gave the effect of slightly raised relief, and which may have made embroideresses realize the potential

The Metropolitan Museum of Art, gift of Mrs. Thomas Watson

*Now in the Bodleian Library, Oxford.

The Bible in embroidered crimson velvet presented to Queen Elizabeth I. *Bodleian Library*

A book of prayers, handwritten by Elizabeth I as a child, with a cover embroidered by her in silver and light blue. A New Year's gift to her stepmother, Queen Katherine Parr. The pansies are padded and raised. *Bodleian Library*

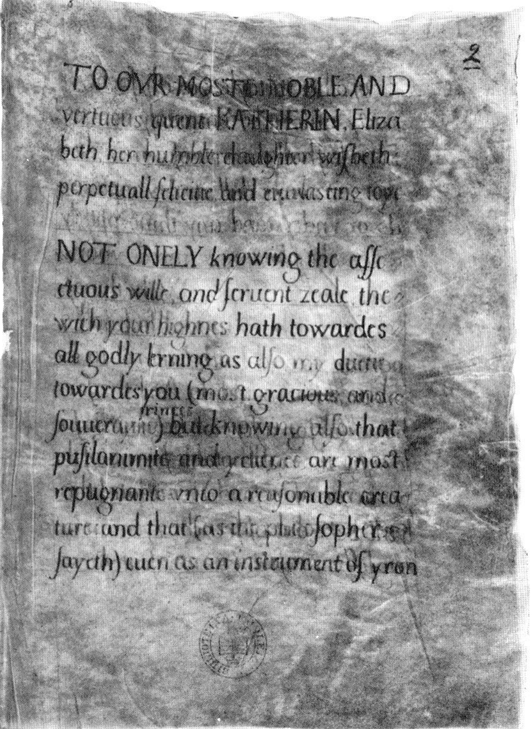

2

TO OVR MOST NOBLE AND
vertuous quene KATHERIN, Eliza
beth her humble daughter wisheth
perpetuall felicitie and everlasting ioye
[illegible]
NOT ONELY knowing the affe
ctuous wille, and feruent zeale the
wich your highnes hath towardes
all godly lerning as also my duetie
towardes you (most gracious and
souueraine princes) but knowing also that
pusilanimite and ydlenes are most
repugnante vnto a reasonable crea
ture and that (as the philosopher
sayeth) euen as an instrument of yron

of three-dimensional work, was the fashion for applying needlepoint canvas to velvet. This innovation, possibly brought to England by Mary Queen of Scots, cleverly avoided the tedium of many hours spent in embroidering the canvas background. Beautifully stylized flowers and plants, just like the cuttings or "slips" which would be used to propagate shrubs and plants in the new gardens, were worked first in petit point in silk and then applied to velvet or silk material and finally edged and connected with gold threads. The novel idea of cutting out the canvas work and applying it to a soft material was particularly suitable for curtains surrounding four-poster beds because not only was it quicker, but the glow of velvet and gold contrasted beautifully with the completely worked needlepoint valances around the top of the bed. Several hangings and long cushions, done in this way by

Needlepoint slips appliquéd on velvet and outlined with gold thread. *The Metropolitan Museum of Art, Rogers Fund, 1920*

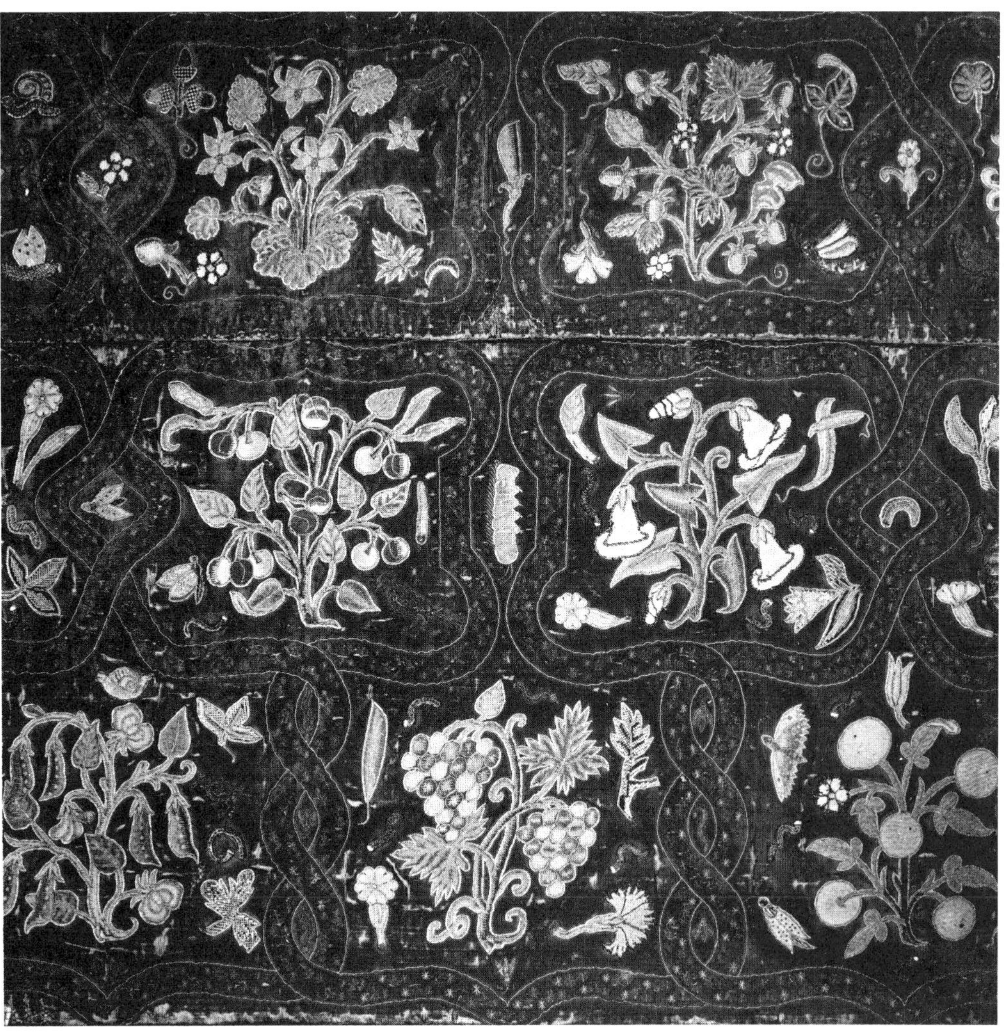

Italian lace in buttonhole stitch with free-standing details. Figures standing on hollie point ground. *Victoria and Albert Museum*

Left front of a bodice. The flowers are in trellis stitch, very similar to hollie point. *The Metropolitan Museum of Art, Rogers Fund, 1923*

Mary Queen of Scots, with the help of the "broudistars" or embroiderers she brought from France, still remain at Hardwick Hall in England to this day.

A letter written in 1656 describes how the work was done:

> But as for the Carpet and Chayr and stoole, I should despayre of seeing an end of them if John Best had not found out a way to ease my wife. But now John takes these borders which my mother wrought and cutts out every single Flower and Leafe, and when they are so voyded, he draws some Turning Stalkes for my wife to work, upon which he will so place the Flowers and Leaves that it shall seem as if all had been wrought together and be perfectly suitable to the pattern on the Bedd.

The fashion for needlepoint lace was a third inspiration to the embroideress about to embark on her raised work masterpiece. This Italian lace, done with a needle in many forms of buttonhole stitch, was made fashionable in France by Catherine de Medici, to whom Vinciolo dedicated his book of needle lace patterns in 1587.

One closely worked version of buttonhole lace was hollie point, a needle lace made entirely of buttonhole stitch. The background of the pattern was solid, made by working the stitches close together, and the design itself was outlined by open holes formed by working the stitches wider apart. Was it called hollie point because of these holes, or because this early form of lace may have been of Arab origin and was brought from the Holy Land? No one is really sure. It was this stitch, when closely worked in silk to resemble petit point, which became the ideal close covering for the raised parts of the stump work designs. See opposite.

Hollie point is one of the stitches used in stump work whose name we recognize today; trellis, twisted braid, bullion knots, and couching are others. But many, listed under "The School Mistris Terms of Art for all her ways of sowing," in an English encyclopedia of 1686, have vanished. What are the smarting Whip stitch, the Finny stitch, the Virgin's Device, the needlework Pearl, the Mow stitch, or the Bread stitch? The names alone inspire us to heights of fancy as to their actual appearance, just as we wonder about such mysterious hues as murray, tawnye, ladies blushe, pound cythrone, or horse flesh, colors which must have rivaled in brilliance their exotic names.

The same encyclopedia also catalogues "terms and things to work with" in the art and skill of stump work, including

Needles of several sizes	Slave silk
Cruel of all colours	Naples silk
Silk sowing of all colours	Fin white Alcomy Wyre
A Tent	Ising Glass
A samcloth, a cloth to sew on	Gum Arabic
A Canvice cloth	

Somehow, the naïveté of the English stump work with its formal treatment of stylized figures, plants, and animals gives it a certain charm and quaintness. Some of the later designs, however, became more and more flamboyant, eventually imitating sculpture to such a degree that whole gardens were made free-standing with the use of wire and other threads. Gathering dust through the ages, their sparkling gold and silver tarnished to a dull charcoal color, these products of so much effort and dedication can only fascinate us today with the delicacy and variety of their stitchery. But occasionally one beautifully preserved piece will fortify our imagination as to what the others must have been. Such a one is a small cabinet in the Metropolitan Museum of Art (opposite).

Another magnificent example is a sixteenth-century English bodice known as the Devereux heirloom. Worked on cloth of silver entirely in gold, silver, and silk thread, with a twining design of roses, iris, carnations, peapods, cornflowers, columbine, and forget-me-nots, all interspersed with caterpillars, birds, and butterflies, it really combines the techniques of canvas, silk and crewel embroidery, as well as raised work. The stitches used are Gobelin and tent as well as buttonhole and chain, using silver and gold wire. The bodice was said to have been sent to Queen Elizabeth by the Countess of Leicester when her son, the Earl of Essex, was awaiting execution in the Tower of London.

Incidentally, this was not the only gift of embroidery designed to soften Elizabeth's heart, for Mary Queen of Scots was always planning to this end. As the ambassador reported to the French king: "The Queen of Scots, your sister-in-law, is very well, and yesterday, I presented on her behalf a skirt of crimson satin worked with silver, very fine, and all worked with her hand, to the Queen of England, to whom the present was very

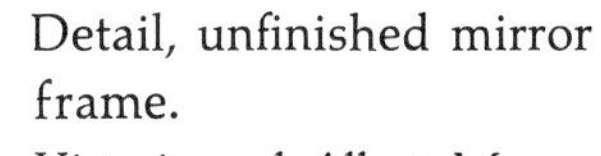

Detail, unfinished mirror frame.
Victoria and Albert Museum

17th-century stump work box illustrating the Five Senses. Appliquéd petit point on ivory satin, enriched with black pearls and coral beads. *The Metropolitan Museum of Art, Rogers Fund, 1929*

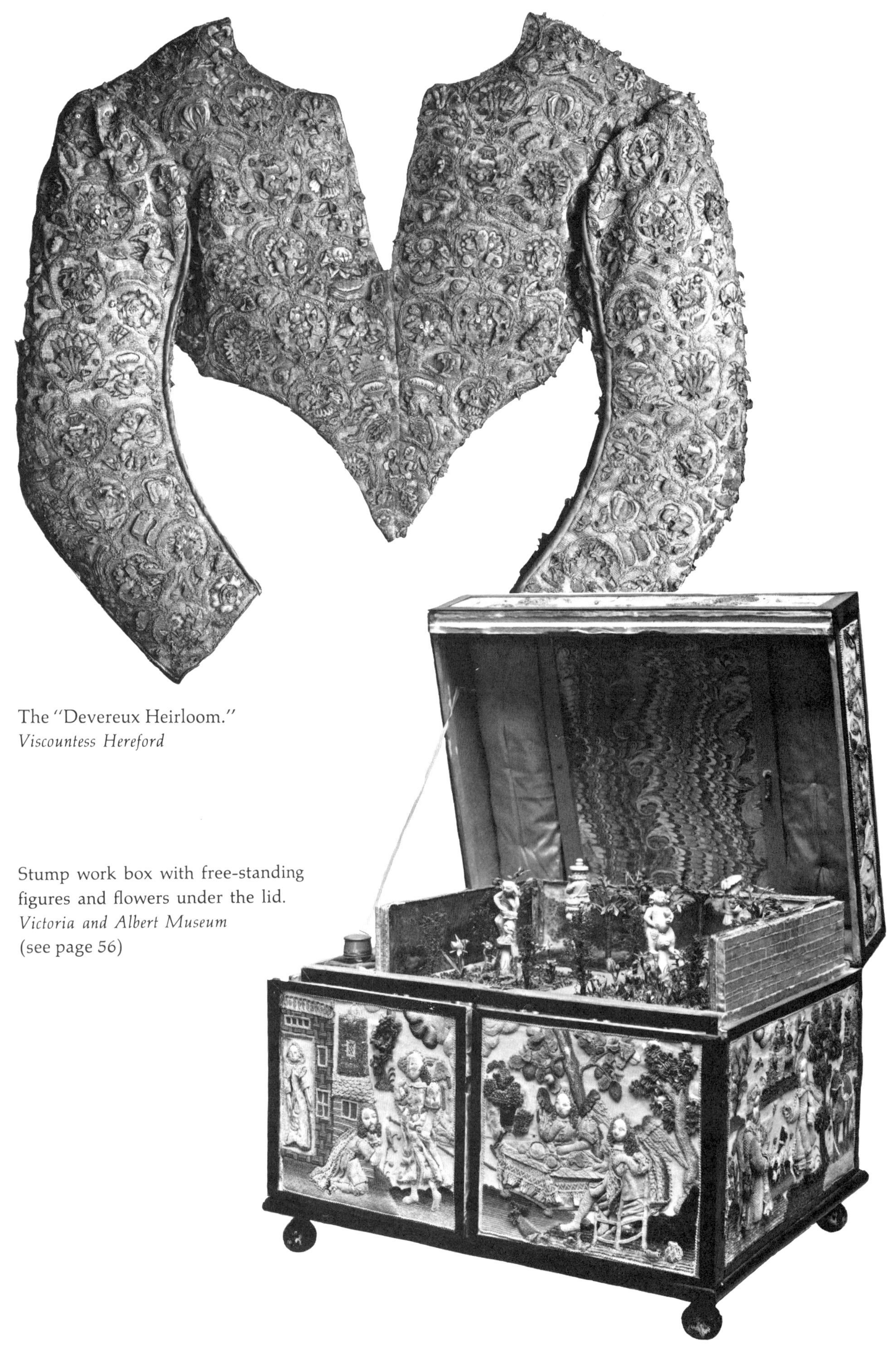

The "Devereux Heirloom."
Viscountess Hereford

Stump work box with free-standing figures and flowers under the lid.
Victoria and Albert Museum
(see page 56)

Worked about 1900 by Mrs. Richard Aldrich (neé Margaret Livingston Chanler). *Courtesy of Mrs. Byron DeMott.*

agreeable for she found it very nice and has prized it much, and it seems to me I found her much softened towards her." Unfortunately for Mary, and for the Countess of Leicester, this laborious handiwork and the ambassador's high hopes were for nought, for while Elizabeth's heart may have been softened, her resolve was rarely undone.

Still another charming piece is an unfinished mirror frame in the Victoria and Albert Museum. Since the frame is in this state, it is possible to get an idea of how the shapes were gradually built up. The stitches are trellis, long and short, couching, bullion knots, and padded satin, with appliqués of embroidered satin and rice stitch on canvas (see page 68).

Tastes change. Toward the end of the 1700's, for an unknown reason, the fashion of stump work suddenly vanished, never to appear in the same form again. Its nearest counterpart, however, would be the raised wool embroidery of the Victorian era, which is fascinating in its own way and considerably bolder in its technique, since it uses only wool threads.

Raised wool embroidery became very popular in the United States as well as in Europe, which is interesting because so few examples of the earlier stump work with silk and metal threads have been found in

America (page 71). This may have been because of the difficulty in obtaining the suitable materials in the eighteenth century, for while the English lady was stitching with imported silk and gold threads, the Colonial embroideress was spinning and dyeing her own wool and weaving her own linen for crewelwork.

When in the nineteenth century the colorful Berlin wool work became so popular, special sheep were bred in Saxony to provide the correct soft merino wool which could be dyed with jewel colors, and this same wool was also used for the raised embroidery. Pictures with sprays and baskets of flowers done in this manner were mounted in deep shadow boxes so that the glass would not crush the raised stitches. Unfortunately, the wool was beloved by moths, who often managed to penetrate the sealed containers. Unfortunately, too, the wool often has faded, but its mellowed softness today is perhaps more attractive than the original harsh contrasts caused by the newly invented aniline dyes.

Victorian raised wool.
Author's Collection

These raised wool pictures are similar to the designs in Turkey work of the same period. The Turkey work designs were always done on canvas, and the stitching was clipped to follow the modeling of the subject. This was so finely done it often resembled velvet and was sometimes called "plush" stitch instead of Turkey work.

When one realizes that stump work and raised embroidery were the culmination of so many styles and influences, one can see that this combination of different stitches is rather like a historical forerunner of today's mixed media.

Today, stump work is enjoying a revival, but in a form that would be unrecognizable to the ladies who made the original beauty boxes and mirror frames of the seventeenth century. Bold hangings with raised appliqués, and crewel-embroidered panels with all kinds of raised wool stitches, are being done by embroiderers, and painters developing the technique of collage are experimenting with threads and fabrics, so that their medium sometimes overlaps into true embroidery.

The lion and the lamb. Note raised cup stitch flowers (see page 85).
Designed and worked by Wilanna Bristow

TO BEGIN

There are all kinds of possibilities for contemporary stump work; appliquéd fabrics can be raised by padding, raised wool embroidery can be done with stitches such as buttonhole, trellis, and Turkey work, and an almost unlimited variety of three-dimensional embroideries can be made from combinations of both these techniques. You could cover any sort of box, from a magnificent jewel box or sewing cabinet, to a pill box (page 78). Jewelry itself, a very special eyeglass case, a handbag, a mirror frame, a tabletop under glass, or a picture or panel that could become a conversation piece, all can be subjects for the experimental needle.

MATERIALS, THREADS, AND TRANSFERRING THE DESIGN

Because the field is open to such a wide variety of effects, the choice of materials is almost unlimited. Silk, satin, antique satin, felt, or even leather and suede, needlepoint canvas, linen, cotton, and wool may be stitched with silk, wool, cotton, beads, or metal threads. Therefore, all the materials listed for the different techniques in this book may be incorporated in this medium.

In order to raise the fabrics and stitches you will first need muslin for lining the padded area. For the padding itself you can use regular cotton from the drugstore, or the Dacron wadding used for stuffing pillows. Even more resilient is the lamb's wool sold in some drugstores for protecting corns! You can also use felt or string to raise the stitches, as described in gold embroidery on pages 48 and 49.

Transferring the design will depend on the choice of fabrics and therefore you can select the method that seems most suitable from the listing on pages 30-33.

Because the stitches are to be raised, you should work on a square frame or on a hoop frame which is large enough to enclose the whole design. Besides being extremely difficult to push down over the embroidery, a small hoop might crush the padded stitches as you move it from one area of the design to another.

THE STITCHES AND TECHNIQUES

Traditional stump work was done on white satin with fine silken stitches, using gold threads, such as bullion and velvety chenille as well as silks. Faces and hands were raised with wooden molds and all kinds of lacy stitches such as hollie point and trellis, which were raised by paddings, were combined with stitches such as long and short and laid, worked flat on the background material.

Similar to stump work were the Victorian raised wool embroideries with fascinating three-dimensional realism, done with all kinds of raised crewel stitches, such as Turkey work, bullion knots, and padded satin (page 72).

If you take a liberal approach, combining traditional stump work with this raised wool needlework, you can use them both as a basis for all kinds of modern abstract creative stitchery. You can work with the

Adam and Eve have padded bodies; felt, beads, raised wool, and metal thread complete the design. *Designed and worked by the author*

traditional delicate tracery of silk and gold stitchery, or explode the scale of these stitches by substituting the fine threads with bulky wools and cords, making the whole effect unrecognizable in its new textural form.

The most important technique used in stump work is, obviously, padding and stuffing. This can be done in various ways.

You can apply any material to the background fabric, cutting out the shape to be applied a little larger than the design, so that when it is sewn down a "bubble" is formed in the center, which will be filled with the stuffing. Leave enough of the edge unstitched so that you can push a padding of cotton between the two layers of fabric, using the points of your scissors to help you. Push the cotton in firmly, but not so hard that it loses its resilience and becomes packed into solid lumps.

Another variation of padding is sewing down a muslin lining which,

Lamb, showing Pekinese stitch and detail above. *Wilanna Bristow*

after padding, will be completely covered with stitching. These stitches should not be sewn down through the padding, but should closely cover it, lying completely on top. Sewing through the padded area is not only difficult, but might flatten the final effect; therefore detached surface stitches such as weaving, trellis, or buttonhole lace are best for this technique. Apply and pad your muslin exactly as before (applying fabric, above), and try out various detached stitches which cover your padded area, yet remain free from the ground except at the edges. Start with weaving, then try trellis stitch, then hollie point and Greek lace filling.

These are the most basic stitches, but any of the lace stitches based on buttonhole for the close weaving stitches which are detached from the background are suitable for working over a padding (see page 94).

If you want a variety of stitches on your raised fabric, or if you only want to put in details such as features or outlines, embroider them first on a separate piece of material, *then* appliqué this and pad it. You can also apply a finished piece of needlepoint canvas according to the instructions on page 83, and raise this with a padding. Or, if you want to go one step further, you can turn back the edges of these stitched materials and hem or oversew them. Then you can either sew them down to the background material, just like patches, or leave them free-standing, just catching them down where necessary. This can work equally well for the petals of a flower or for an entirely abstract shape in a design.

A further development of this is to stitch your shape so that it may be seen completely in the round, like sculpture. By threading wire inside the shapes you can make them stiff enough to stand up on their own, away from the background. An excellent example of this is "before" and "after" on page 78, showing a caterpillar and a butterfly as the free-standing decoration atop a pair of pillboxes.

Alternatively, you can raise the background fabric from behind, rather like quilting, by basting muslin over the back of your design, stitching closely round the outlines—back stitch is the best (page 92)—and then pushing the padding cotton in between the muslin and the background fabric, from behind.

You can also pad with any of the methods described for gold embroidery, using layers of felt or string and working with either gold, silk, or wool on this raised surface, as you please.

Lady with a Pekinese, needlepoint completely in the round. *Designed and worked by Robert Heitmann*

Ecology panel with flat and padded appliqués and raised stitchery. As the panel was made for six-year-olds in a San Antonio school, the mouse squeaks, the frog croaks, and the possum holds baby possums in a zippered pouch. *Designed and worked by Wilanna Bristow*

RIGHT. Sailor in padded needlepoint appliquéd to a Gobelin stitch background, worked in a bargello pattern. *Designed and worked by Mrs. Carroll O'Connor*

"Before and After" pill boxes. *Designed and worked by Wilanna Bristow*

THE STITCHES

If you want to raise your embroidery by stitching alone, you can use the traditional raised wool work as your inspiration, and, with a lightness of touch which is contemporary, work normally flat crewel stitches in high relief. Page 80 and page 86 show the effect of some of these stitches, which are included in this listing:

Raised seeding	Raised needleweaving
Raised rope stitch	Raised chain (on a raised band)
Looped stem	Raised buttonhole
Raised close herringbone	Raised stem
Puffy couching	Raised spiderwebs
Trellis and raised cup stitch	Ladder stitch

As you see, you can achieve exciting effects by working these stitches, alone or in combination with regular raised crewel stitches, such as padded satin, French knots on stalks, and Turkey work. Alternatively, you can combine them with the smooth texture of flat crewel stitches to give dramatic contrast.

Strawberries in trellis stitch. *Designed and worked by Mrs. William Sloan*

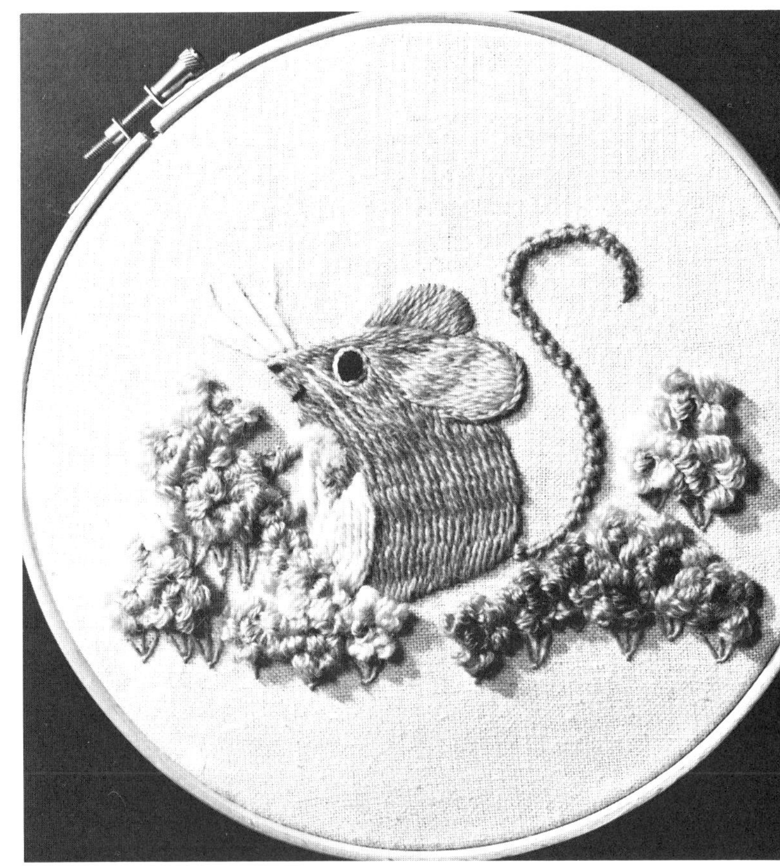

The mouse in plate stitch, tail in knotted pearl, flowers in raised seeding. *Designed and worked by the author*

Raised rope stitch in enlarged detail.
Designed and worked by the author

*PADDED APPLIQUÉ

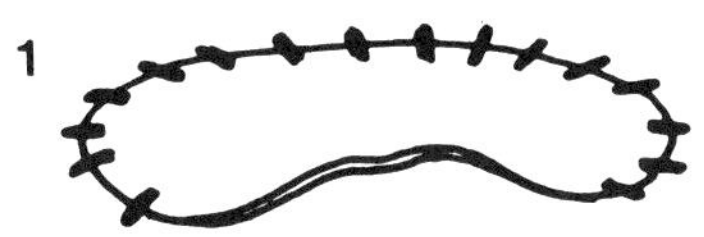

Cut out your shape (slightly larger than your finished area) and apply it to the material, leaving one side open as shown.

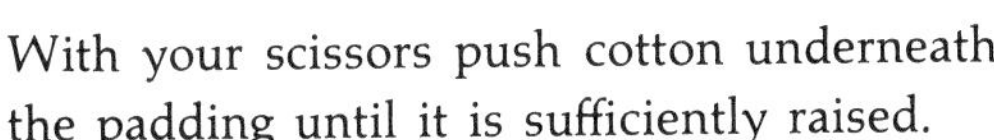

With your scissors push cotton underneath the padding until it is sufficiently raised.

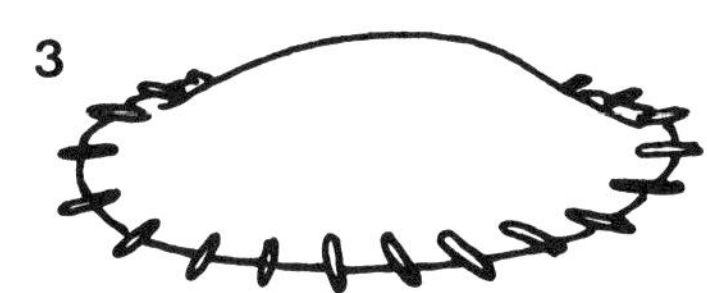

Sew down the open area. The appliqué may then be left as is or covered with another layer of stitching as in #4.

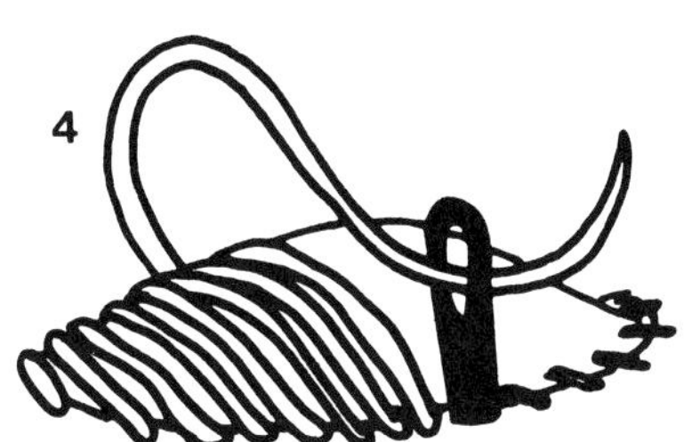

Prepare to weave across the surface by laying threads diagonally across as shown. Do not pull too tightly to destroy the effect of the padding.

Using a blunt needle and starting across the center of the shape weave in the opposite direction. Carefully push threads close together as you weave so that they do not "fall off" the curved surface. Though weaving is shown here, any close stitching may be used to cover raised appliqué, such as trellis, ceylon or raised chain, stem or buttonhole.

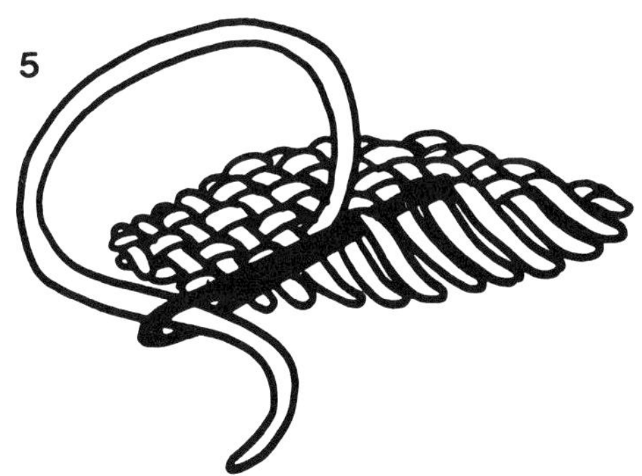

Turkey work cut and uncut. *Designed and worked by Jeri Kilgroe*

*PADDING WITH MUSLIN ON REVERSE SIDE

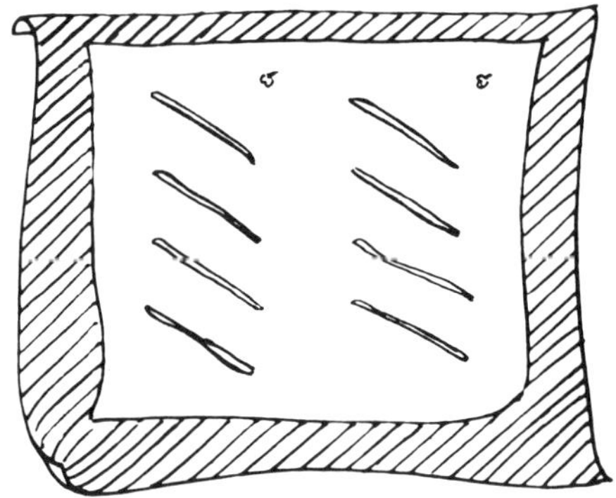

Baste muslin to the reverse side.

Outline your design with back stitch on the right side.

Make a slit in the muslin, push in the cotton, pushing it well into the corners until it is sufficiently padded. Next stitch together the slit in the muslin. Extra muslin may then be trimmed away around the design.

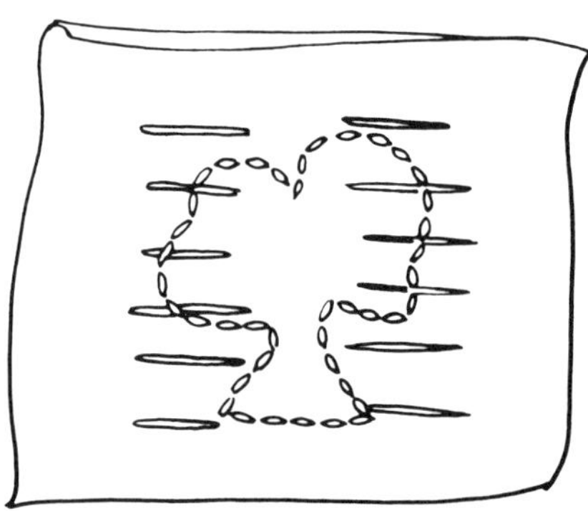

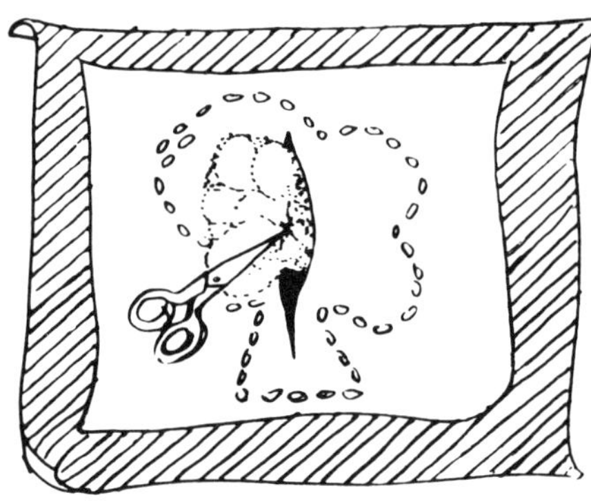

Ferdinand the Bull, under a cork tree with real corks, is embroidered in Turkey work, cut and uncut. *Designed and worked by Jeri Kilgroe*

APPLYING FINISHED NEEDLEPOINT TO FABRIC

First unravel your raw edges around your finished needlepoint so that single threads appear on all four sides as in the diagram. Then pin and baste the needlepoint in position on the background material. With a large-eyed needle take each thread through to the reverse side of the fabric.

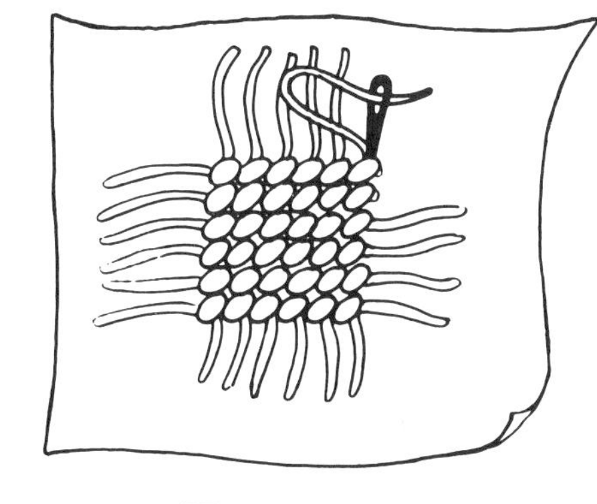

Turn to the reverse side and knot the needlepoint threads together in pairs, pulling snugly so that the canvas is held firmly in place on the front.

Now turn to the right side again and outline the canvas with any edging stitch you prefer. In the diagram, stem stitch is shown at A, couching at B and a couched cord at C. D shows the needlepoint canvas left plain without an edging, which is also equally effective if desired.

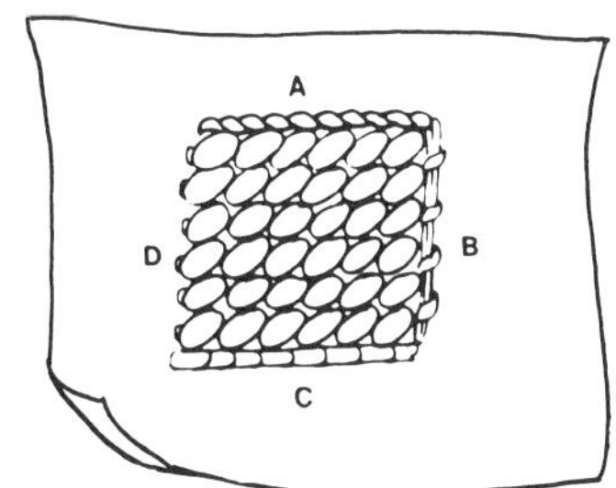

FREE-STANDING STUMP WORK USING WIRE

Embroider shape on fabric.

1
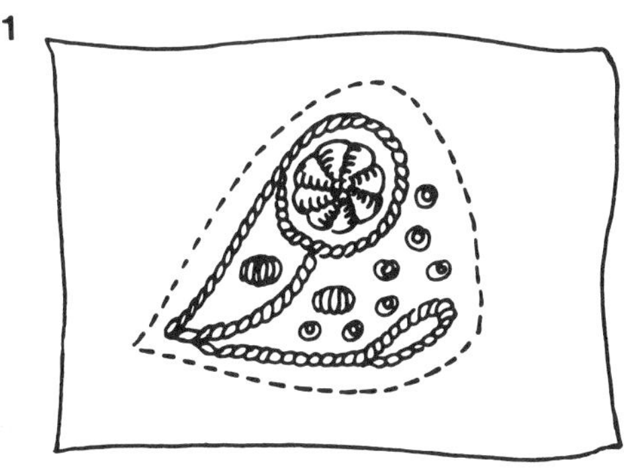

Join it to backing, with right sides facing. Leave one section open (shown by dotted line). Snip notches in the turnbacks for smooth seams and rounded finished edges.

Turn to the right side and insert a loop of wire through the open end. Leave ends of wire long enough to use for attaching to main design.

Attach by taking wire through to the wrong side. Blind stitch the last opening by stitching it together with small invisible stitches. Add final embroidery details (body, etc.).

2
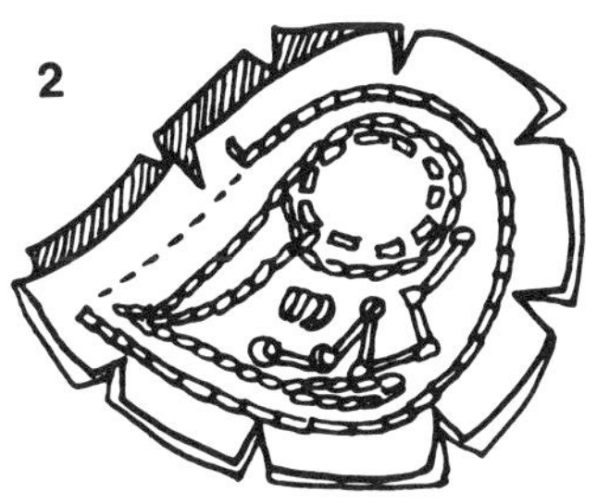

3
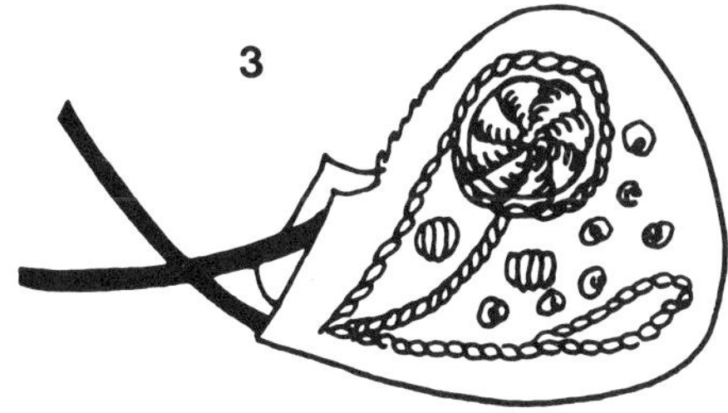

4
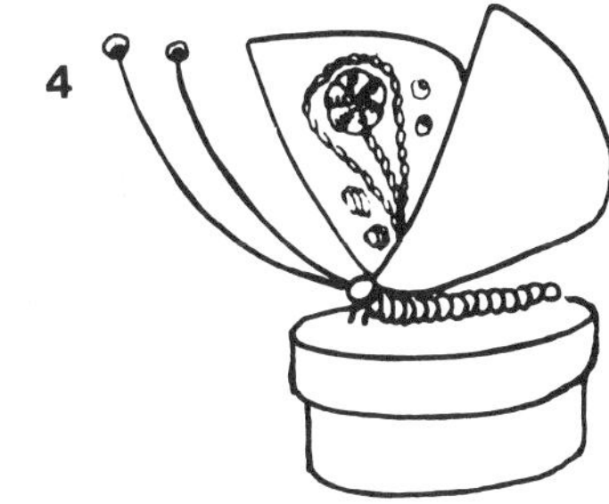

*TRELLIS STITCH

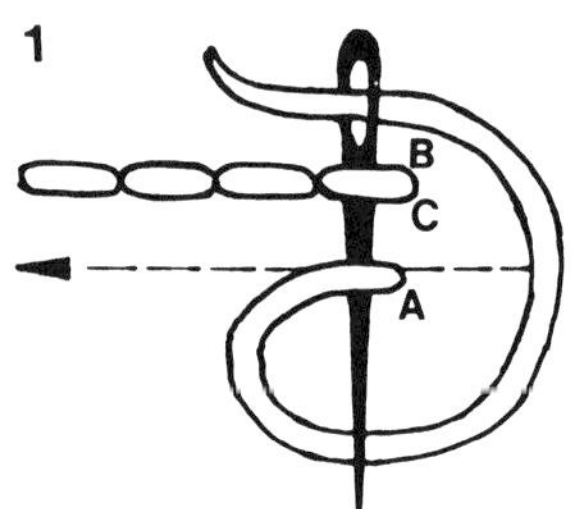

1. Begin with a row of back stitch to make a foundation on which to begin working. Using a blunt tapestry needle, come up on the right at A, immediately below the first back stitch (page 92).

2. Slide the needle vertically under this first back stitch, and then fold the working thread (which comes out of the fabric at A), first over the needle, and then under it, as shown. Draw gently through and pull up to form a knot.

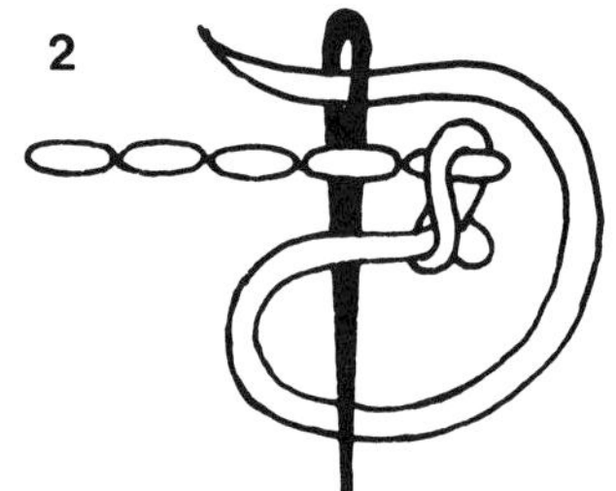

3. Continue, repeating this stitch to the end of the line. Go into the material at D, and taking a vertical stitch, the size of one knot, come up at E.

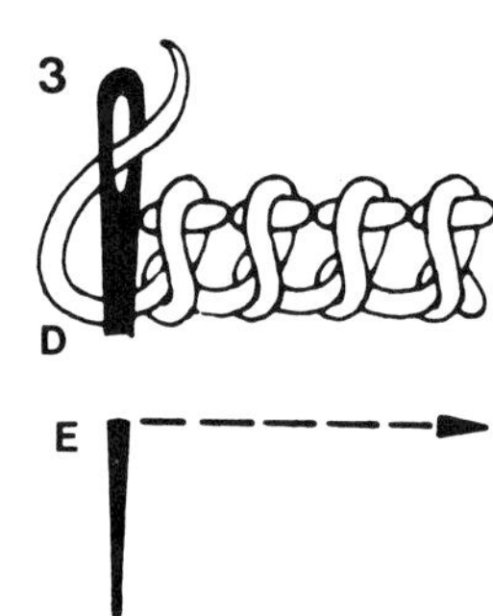

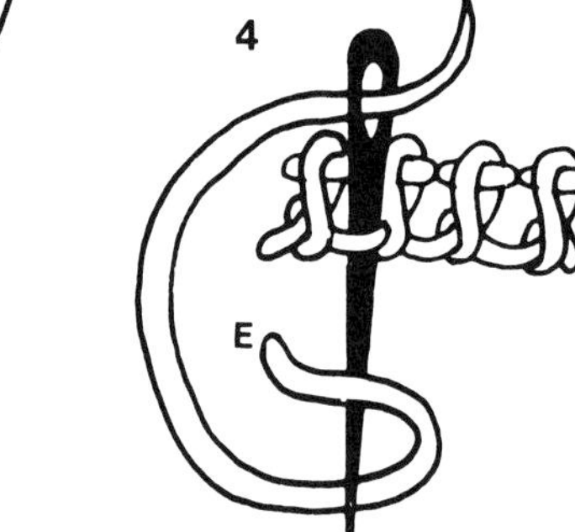

4. Now, work from left to right, repeating the first line, but in the opposite direction, slipping the needle under the bars which connect each stitch.

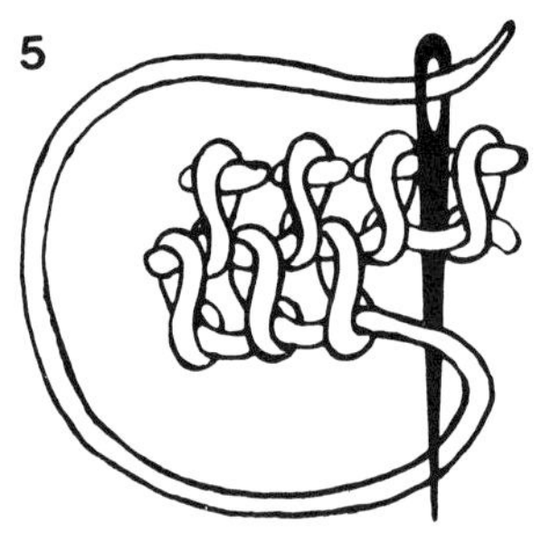

5. Work to the end of the row, drawing each stitch up gently to make an even row of knots.

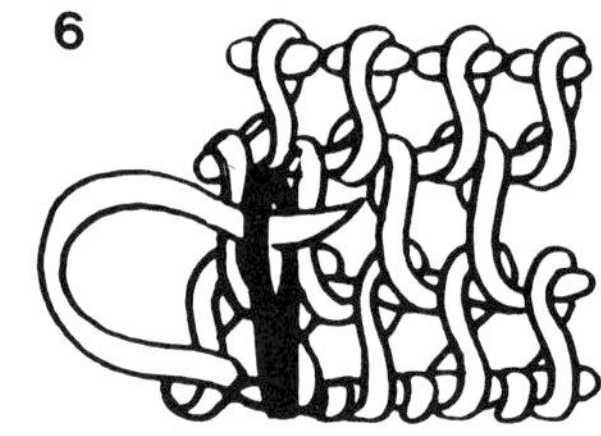

6. Finally, anchor the last line by taking a small stitch over each bar of the last row.

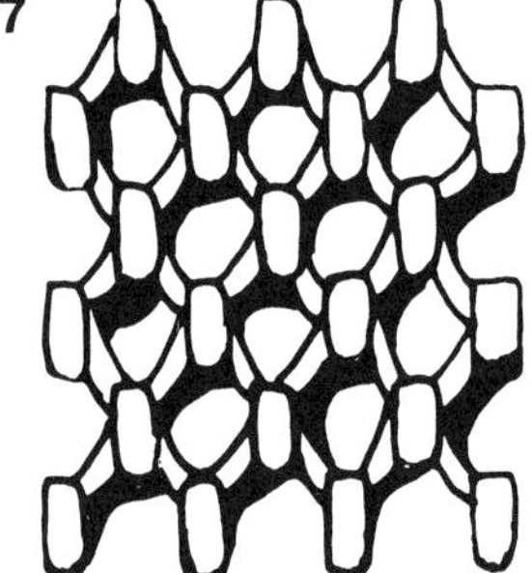

The effect of trellis can vary tremendously according to tension. If you stretch out the finished web the final effect is as shown here.

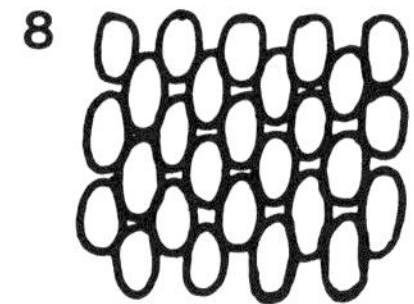

If you work very closely, the knots make a solid covering. Trellis may be worked in horizontal rows, or in curved lines to fit any shape. Alternatively, the whole shape may be outlined with back stitch, then decreasing rows of trellis may be worked round and round inside as shown at right. To obtain a raised circle, do not start decreasing the stitches until nearing the center. The stitches will then stand out as though there were padding underneath them. (See lady's sleeves, page 55, and strawberry eyeglass case, page 79.)

*CEYLON STITCH

Using a blunt (tapestry) needle, begin by coming up at A and going down at B to form a base line the width of the shape to be embroidered. (If the distance is wide, hold this stitch down with small stitches at regular intervals across it.)

Now begin the stitch itself, which is always worked from left to right. Come up at C and slip the needle under the base stitch from D to E and over the working thread which comes out at C. Do not go through the material.

Make a second stitch to the right, exactly like #2, and continue, repeating these stitches to the end of the line.

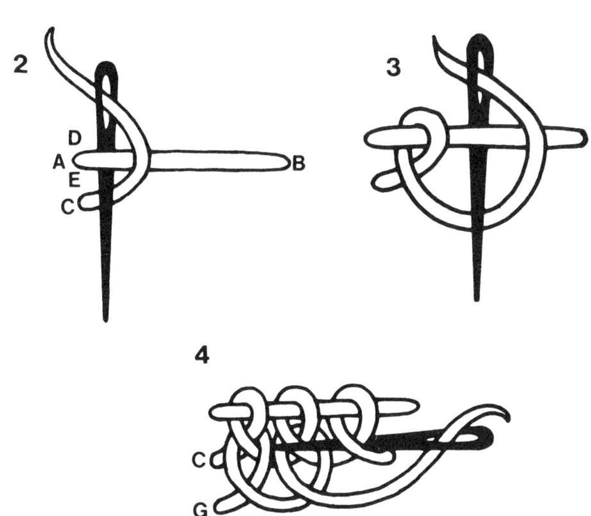

Now come up on the left at G, immediately below C, and slip the needle behind first loop of the previous row, from H to J. Slide horizontally under two threads, where one loop overlaps another, as shown.

Continue, repeating #4 to the end of the line. Secure the final row with small stitches taken through each loop, into the material. The shape may be increased or decreased by adding or taking away stitches at the end of each row.

*RAISED CUP STITCH

Make a triangle of 3 back stitches, in the center of the area to be worked.

Using a blunt (tapestry) needle, slide under one back stitch. Do not go through the material. Take the thread over the needle, then under it as shown.

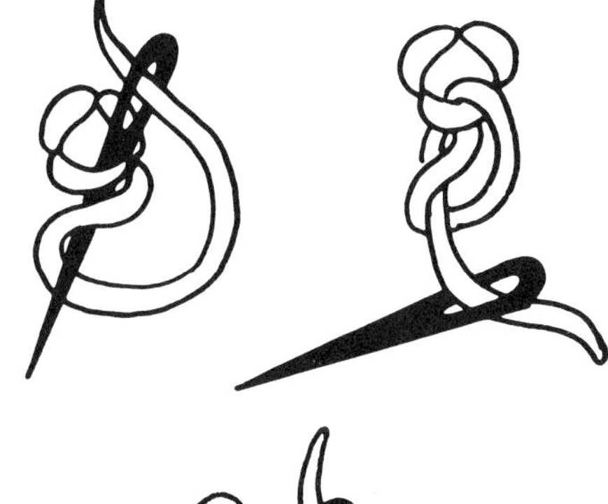

Pull through gently to form a knot.

Repeat, making a second knot beside the first one on the same bar. Pull through, gently.

Puffy couching, Turkey work, French knots on stalks and raised stem stitch give a three-dimensional effect. *Designed and worked by the author*

Continue, making two knots on each bar to make a complete ring around the back stitches. Then make a second ring of stitches by sliding the needle under the bar between each knot (at arrow).

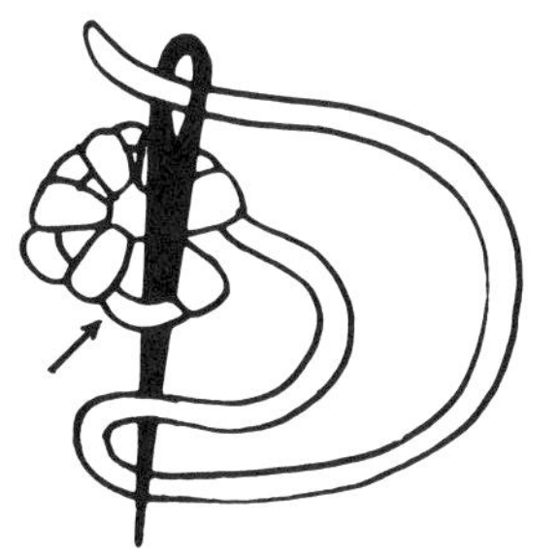

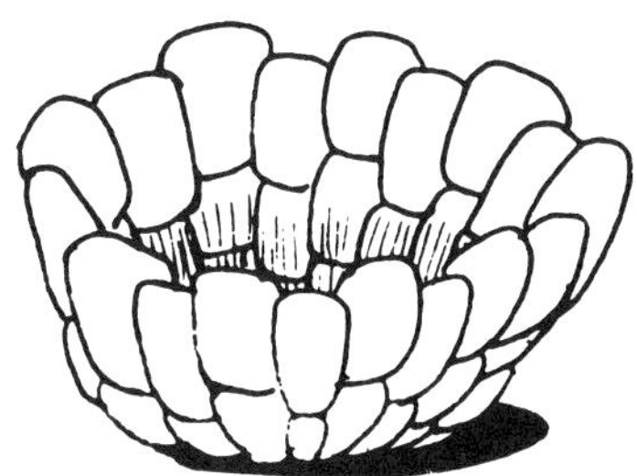

Work round and round, if necessary occasionally working two knots into the bars to increase the size of the cup.

Finished effect (See flowers on tree, page 55.)

*LOOPED STEM

Work lines of regular stem stitch (see page 93) but use heavy thread and leave each stitch loose to form a loop, as shown. The thickness of the thread worked into a fairly fine linen will hold the loops firmly in place. (See page 55, grass under lady's feet.)

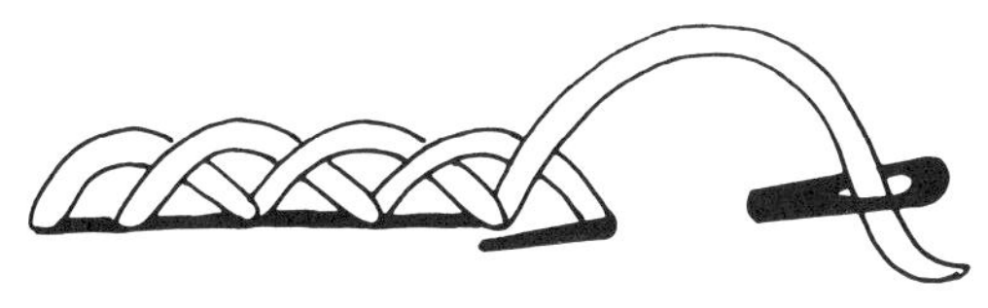

*RAISED ROPE

Work rope stitch (see page 93) but leave the stitches loose to form a raised ridge. This is particularly effective when worked in a circle. (See page 80, close-up of rope stitch flower in vase.)

*RAISED SEEDING

Work seeding (see page 92) but leave each stitch loose to form a raised "bump" on the fabric. As in looped stem the thickness of the thread will hold the seed stitch in place. (See page 79, mouse with flowers.)

PUFFY COUCHING

Work a line of couching (see page 37), but instead of laying the threads flat on the fabric, lift them with your needle as you take each couching stitch to form the raised look shown opposite.

*RAISED CLOSE HERRINGBONE

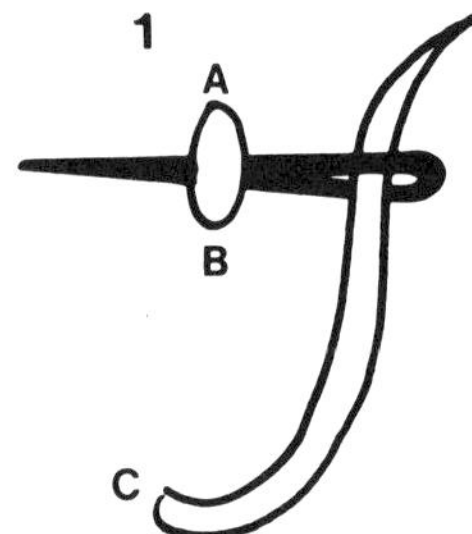

Come up at A, go down at B, making a small vertical stitch at the top of the shape. Then come up at C, slightly to the left at the base. Using a blunt needle, slide through stitch AB from right to left. Do not go through the material.

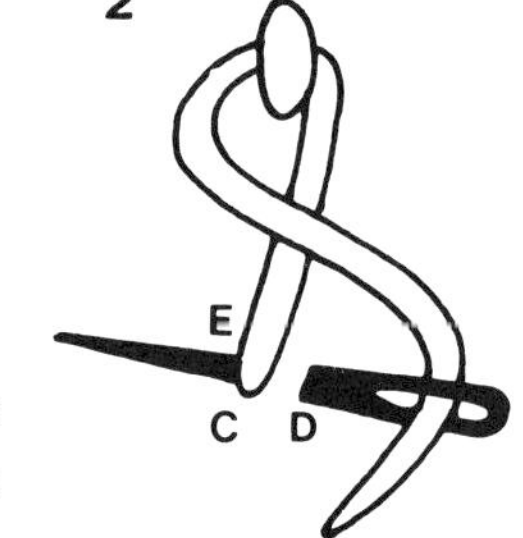

Go into the fabric at D, slightly to the right at the base, and come up at E, immediately above C on the outline of the shape.

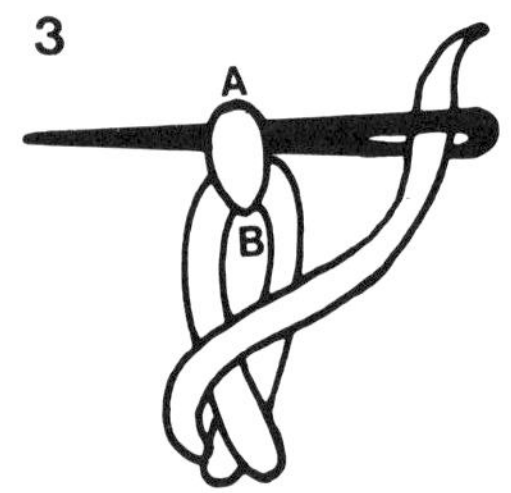

Slide through stitch AB from right to left again, taking care that the stitches lie smoothly side by side.

Go into the material at the base again, going down on the right, and up on the left, just above the other stitches.

Continue, repeating 2, 3, and 4 to the top to make a raised leaf.

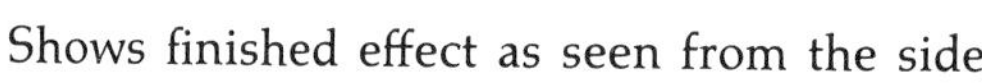

Shows finished effect as seen from the side.

*RAISED NEEDLEWEAVING

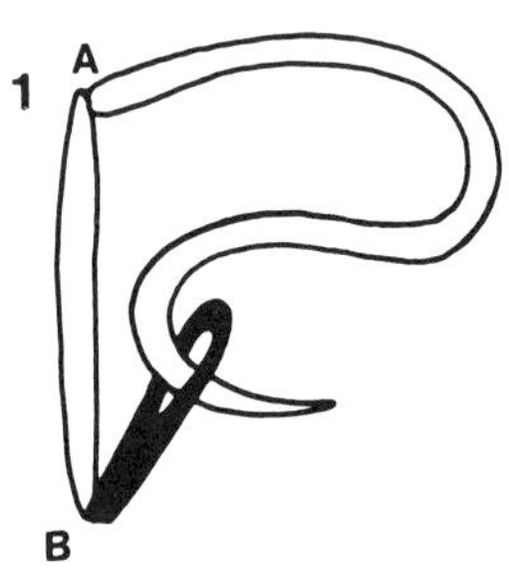

Using a blunt needle, come up at A, down at B, and repeat, coming up at A, down at B again, so that two stitches lie side by side. Do not draw too tight.

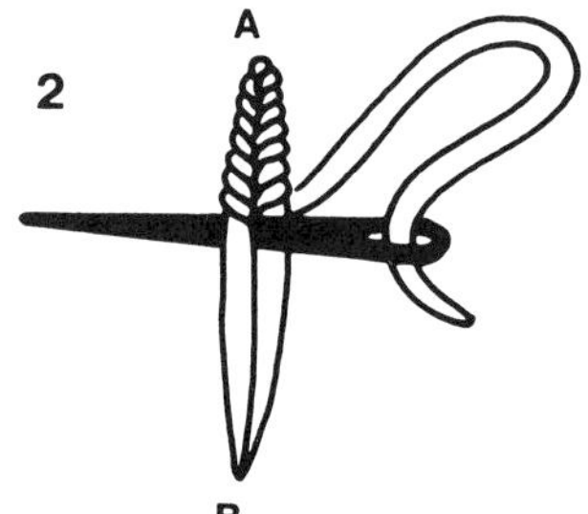

Coming up at A once more, start to weave (without going through the material). First pick up the left hand thread, pushing the needle through from right to left.

Then pick up the right hand thread, pushing the needle through from left to right. Continue till the two underlying threads are completely covered. From time to time pack the weaving threads together by pushing them up with the needle. Keep the tension even so that the line will be smooth.

*RAISED SPIDER'S WEBS

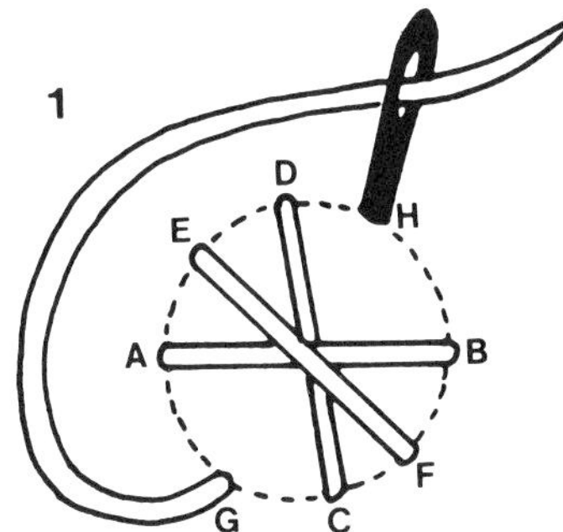

Using a blunt (tapestry) needle, come up at A, down at B, across center of circle.

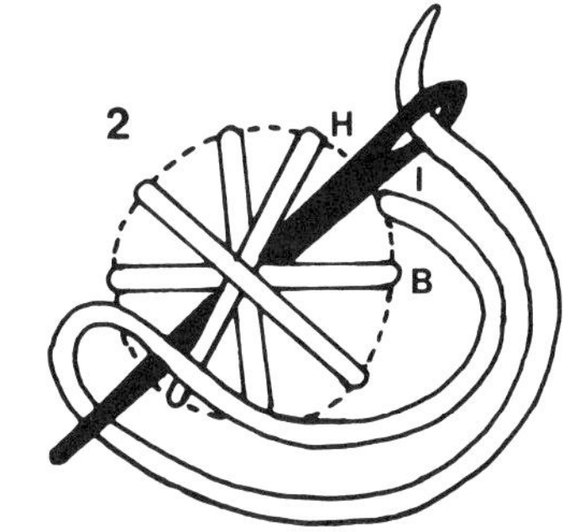

Then come up at C, and down at D (C to D should be slightly off center as shown). Come up at E, down at F, up at G, and down at H. (H goes in quite close to D.)

Pulling the knotting thread upwards, take another blunt needle threaded with any contrasting color and push it under all the spokes.

This leaves a space for the needle to come up finally at I, a point midway between H and B. Then slide the needle under all the threads at their intersection. Take the thread and loop it across the needle and then under it as shown. Draw through and pull upwards to knot threads together in center.

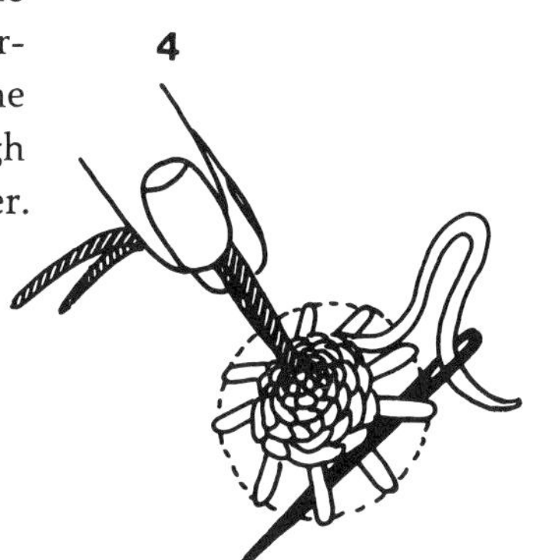

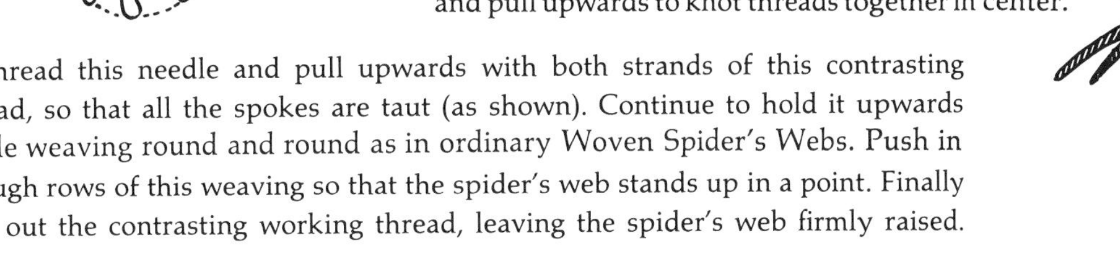

Unthread this needle and pull upwards with both strands of this contrasting thread, so that all the spokes are taut (as shown). Continue to hold it upwards while weaving round and round as in ordinary Woven Spider's Webs. Push in enough rows of this weaving so that the spider's web stands up in a point. Finally pull out the contrasting working thread, leaving the spider's web firmly raised.

*RAISED BUTTONHOLE

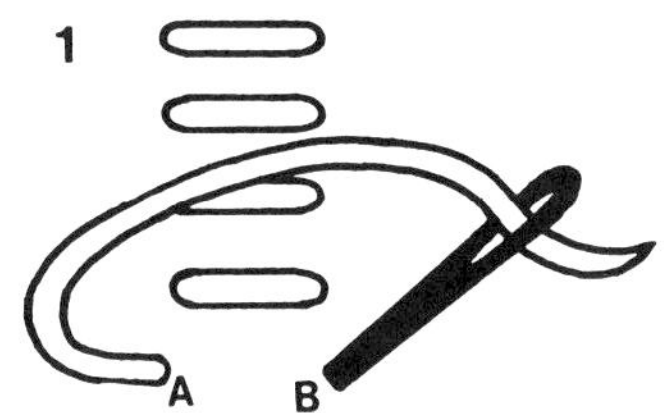

Using a blunt needle, come up at A, form a loop with the thread, and without going through the material, slide under the first bar from B to C (as shown). Draw down towards you until the thread is snug. This forms a buttonhole stitch on the horizontal bar.

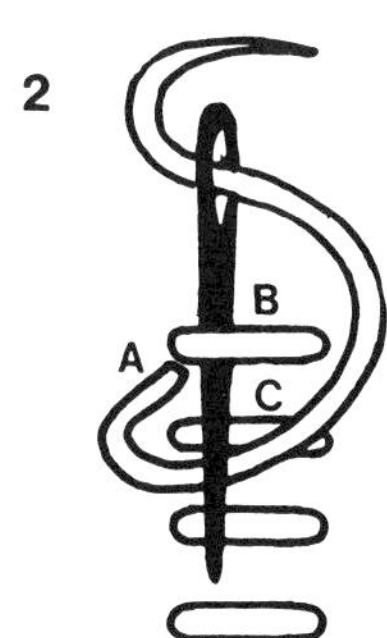

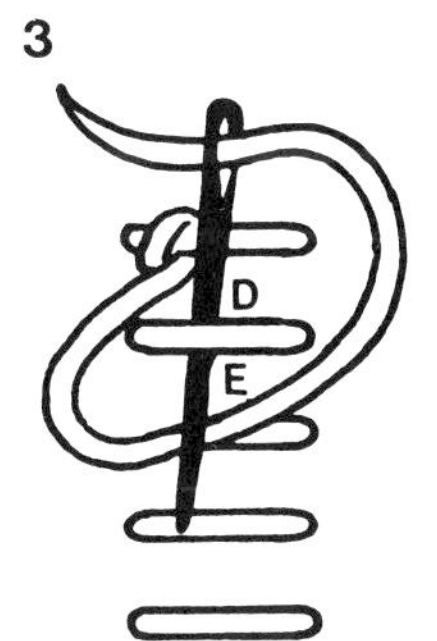

Repeat #2, sliding the needle under the thread from D to E, and work to the bottom of the bars in this way. When you have reached the bottom of each line, anchor the final stitch by going down through the material over the buttonhole loop at F (as in diagram #4).

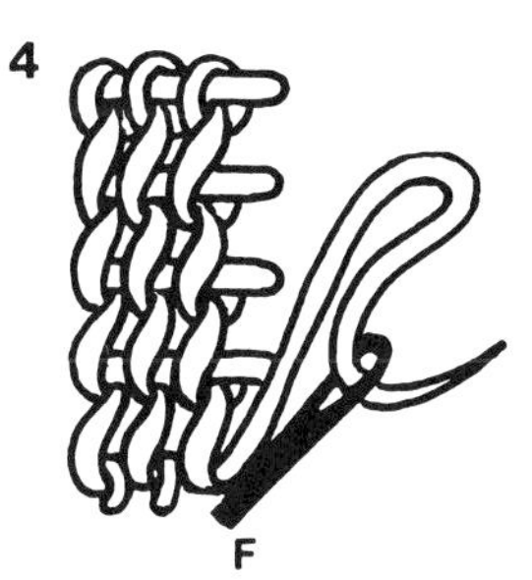

Work several lines close side by side, always beginning at the top, working downwards, until the bars are entirely covered. Do not pack too many rows in or the effect will be lost.

*RAISED BUTTONHOLE ON A RAISED BAND

(Raised buttonhole is shown here, but any of the stitches worked on bars, such as raised stem or chain, may be worked on raised bands.)

1

2

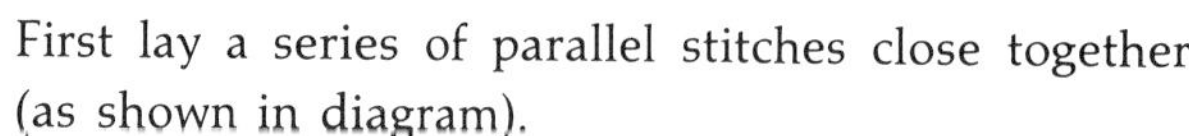

First lay a series of parallel stitches close together (as shown in diagram).

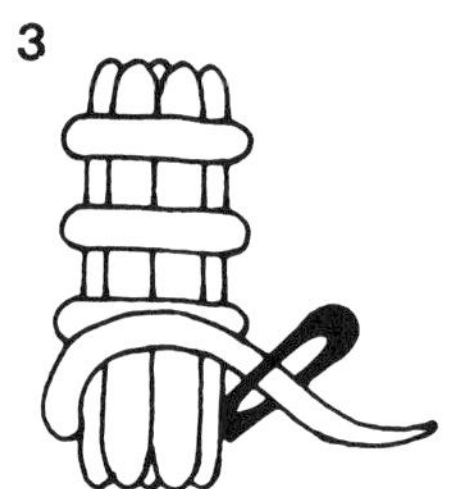

Lay a second row of stitches over the first, keeping the stitches away from the edges. Several decreasing rows may be worked in this way so that the band has a raised center.

Lay a series of parallel stitches across the band just under $\frac{1}{4}$" apart (as shown in diagram).

4

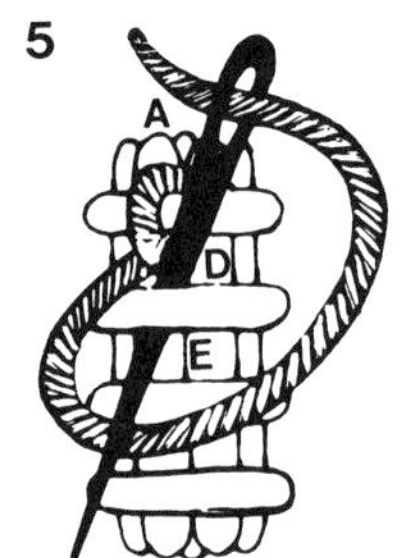

Using a blunt needle, come up at A, form a loop with the thread, and without going through the material, slide under the first bar from B to C (as shown). Draw down towards you until the thread is snug. This forms a buttonhole stitch on the horizontal bar.

Repeat #4 sliding the needle under the thread from D to E and work to the base of the bar in this way. When you have reached the base of each line, anchor the final stitch by going down through the material over the buttonhole loop at F (as in diagram #6).

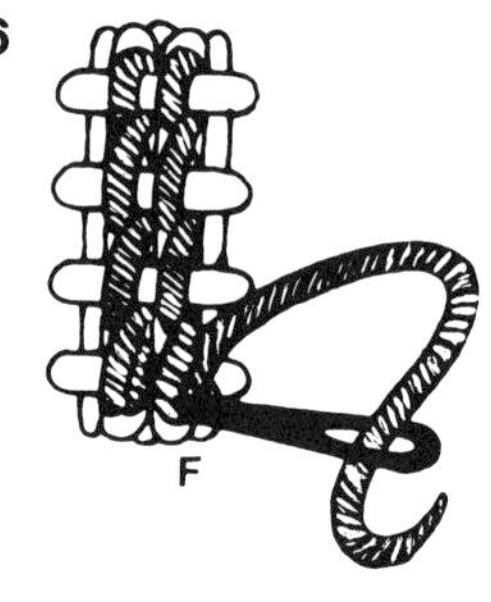

SNAIL TRAIL

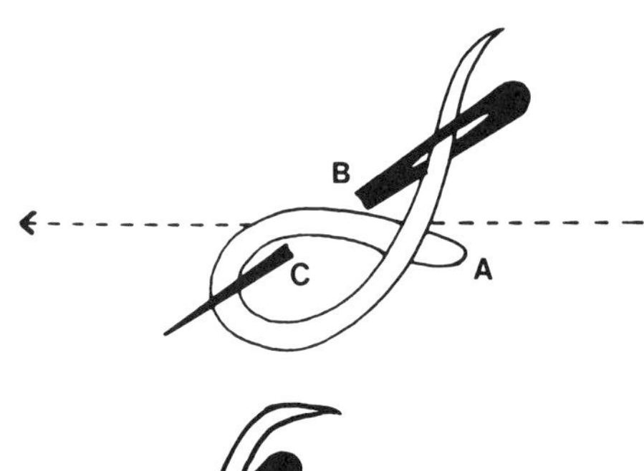

Working from right to left, come up at A. Lay the wool flat along the line you are working (you can hold it in place with your thumb) and take a large slanting stitch across this line from B to C. Before pulling through, twist the wool first over, then under the needle as shown.

Shows finished effect with fairly large stitches spaced wide apart. The effect is entirely different if you change the slant of the needle and the spacing of the stitches. Snail trail worked very close becomes Broad Rope stitch. When worked with the needle at right angles to the thread, instead of slanting, it becomes Coral.

*ROSE LEAF STITCH

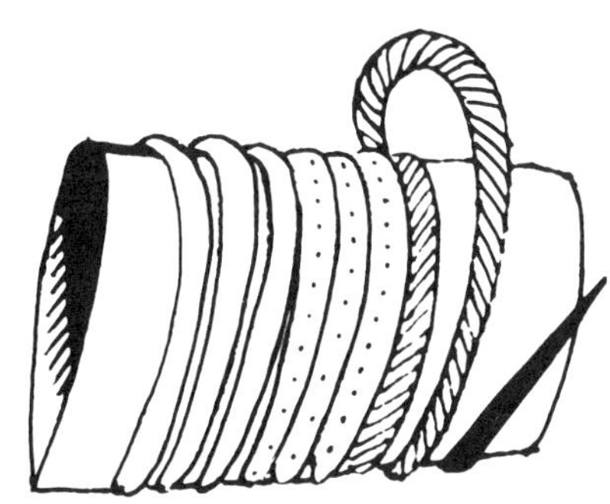

Double a piece of cardboard (postcard is good) so that it measures the size you want your loops to be (from one to two inches is a good average size, but it will depend on the thickness of the yarn and the scale of the design). Mount the work in a frame and hold the card in place along the center of the leaf shape. Using knitting worsted or a single strand of any bulky wool, come up on one side, go over the cardboard and down on the other. Go down close beside where you came up, but not in the same hole. Make three light-colored stitches side by side, three medium and three dark.

Slide the cardboard out.

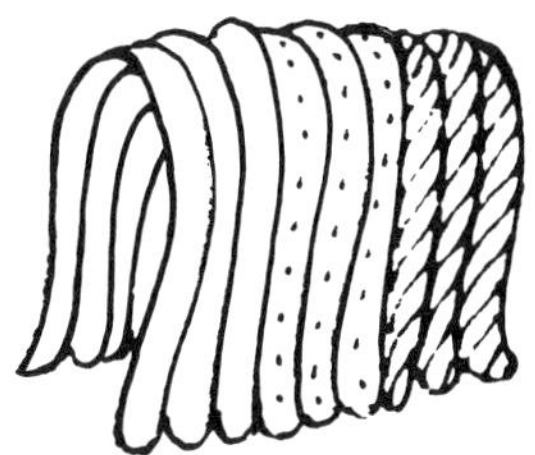

Carefully turn the loops inside out, pushing the dark ones through the light, so that when twisted the loops form a leaf or petal shape, evenly shading from light to dark.

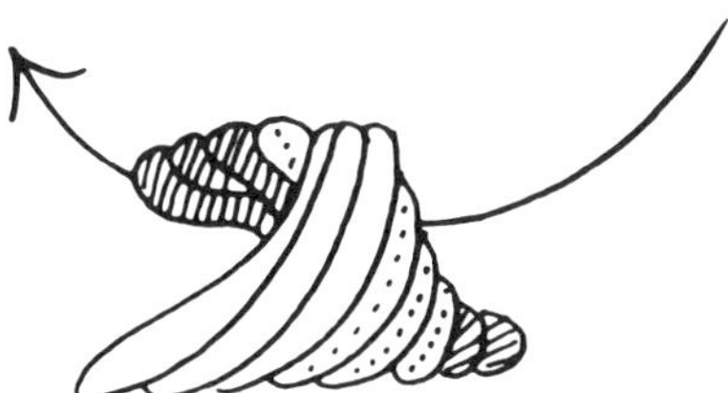

Come up at the end of the shape and sew through the last loop of dark color which has been twisted right through. Go down in the same hole as where you came up, to hold the tip of the leaf.

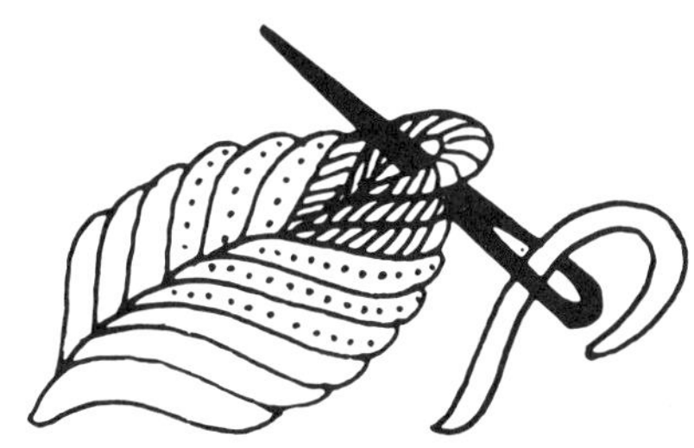

Work one stitch down the middle to form a vein.

Shows the stitch sewn across at the tip to form a rosebud

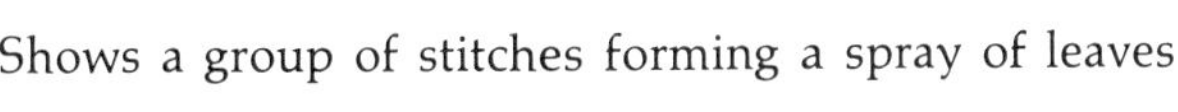

Shows a group of stitches forming a spray of leaves

BACK STITCH

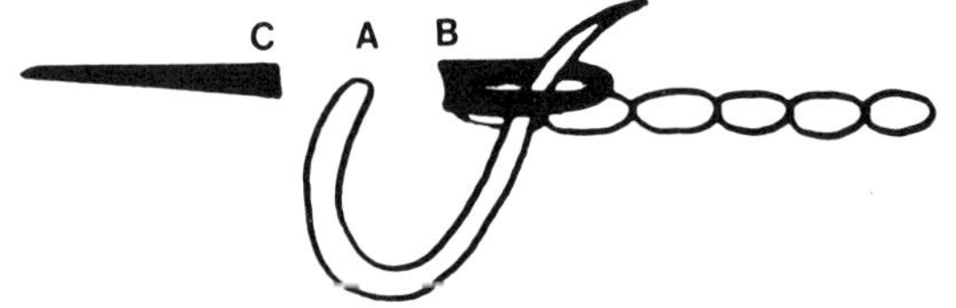

Come up at A, go down at B, then up ahead at C. Repeat, going back into same hole as the previous stitch. Keep all stitches the same size.

* SEEDING

Come up at A, and go down at B a small distance away. Pull through, lightly.

Come up at C and go down at D, across the first stitch, diagonally. Pull through, so that the stitch forms a firm, round, slightly raised "bump" on the fabric.

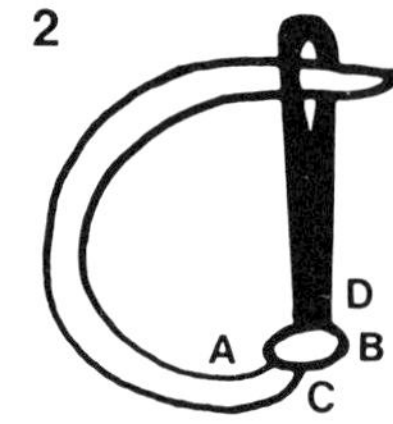

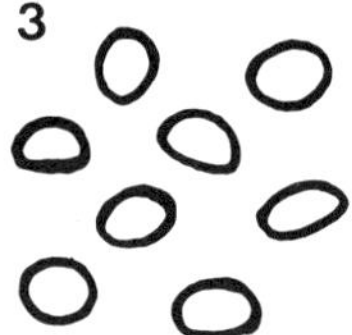

The finished effect appears as one raised stitch instead of two. When worked with thread which matches the background fabric in color seeding gives an attractive textured effect.

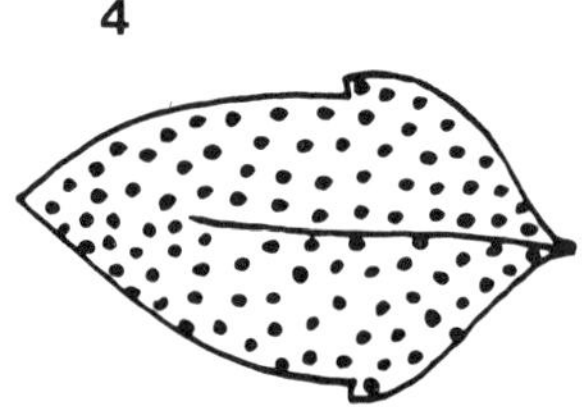

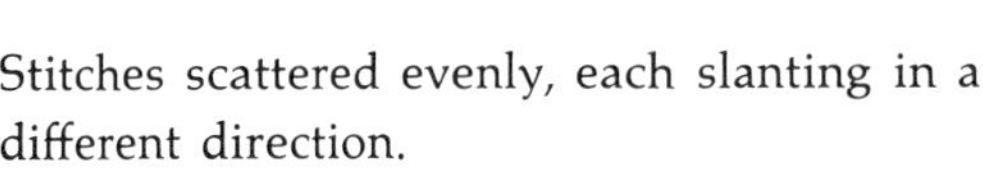

Stitches scattered evenly, each slanting in a different direction.

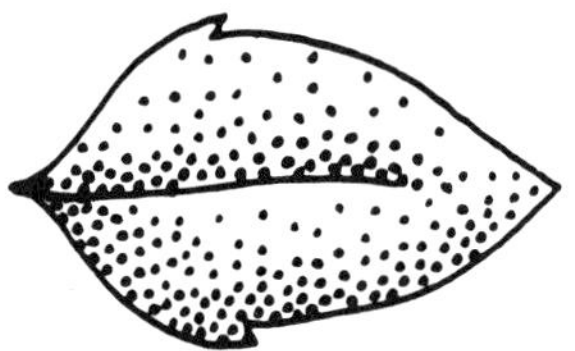

Stitches massed closely to form a shaded effect.

STEM STITCH

Needle comes up at A, goes in at B, and up again at C, exactly halfway between A and B. Draw through, holding the thread to the left of the needle.

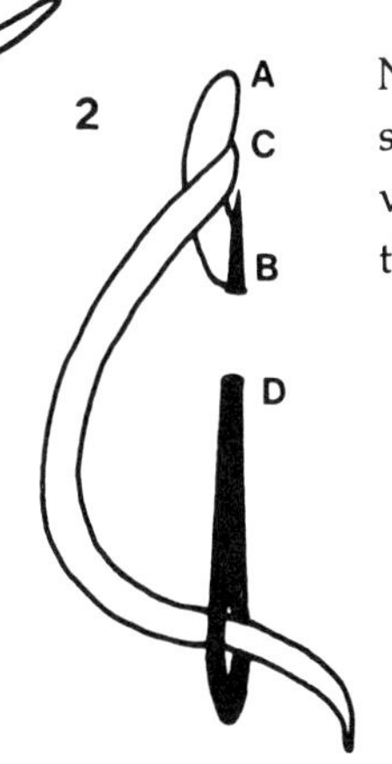

Needle goes in at D, up again at B (in the same hole made by the thread going in previously at B). Draw through, still holding thread to left of needle.

Continue by repeating #2. The thread may be held either to the right or the left of the needle, but should remain on the same side once the work is started.

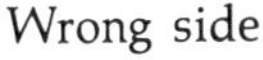

Wrong side

ROPE STITCH/NARROW

This stitch may be used as an outline, or as a solid filling, working the rows close together, all in the same direction. It is difficult to make this stitch smooth without practicing a little first, but it helps if the stitches are fairly long. Use double thread.

Come up at A and go down at B, immediately below A. Form a loop and come up at C, directly below B and inside the loop; draw flat. This stitch is like Chain, except that the thread is crossed in front of the needle before looping under it, and exactly like Rope Stitch-Broad, except that the needle is almost straight, instead of slanting.

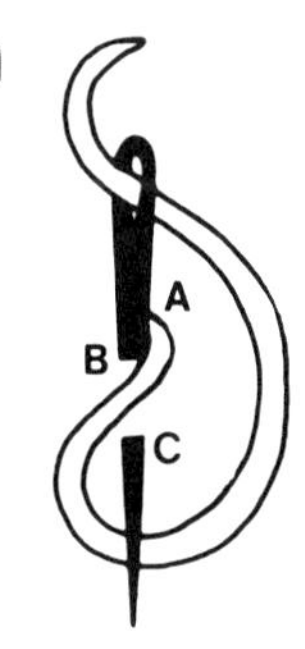

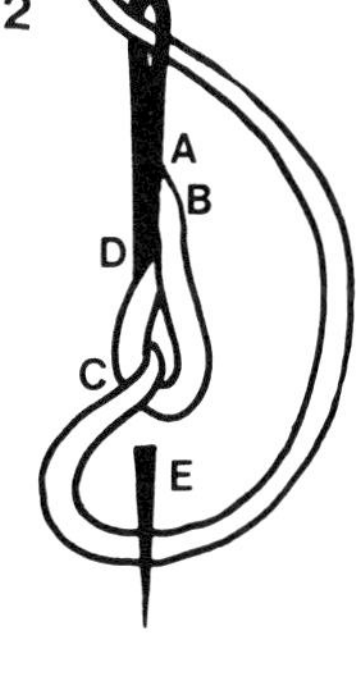

Go down at D, pushing the needle very close up into the waist formed by the twisted chain. Looping the thread under the needle, come up at E on a straight line below A; draw flat.

Repeat #2, and continue along the line. A smooth effect will be gained only if the needle is pushed very close, almost under the stitches (at arrow). The stitch must also be pulled down toward you to tighten it, or the loop will not lie flat.

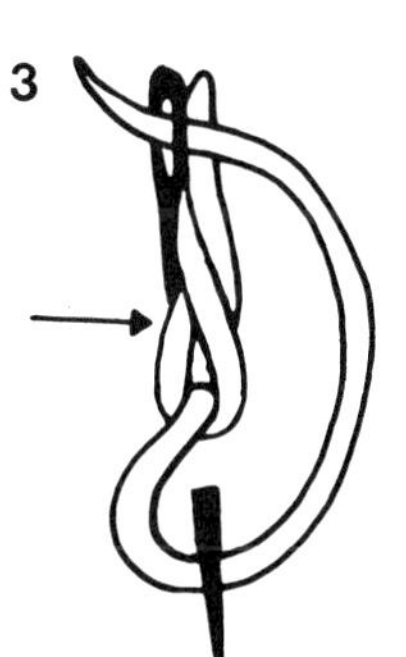

Finished effect

DETACHED BUTTONHOLE FILLING

for Needlemade Lace

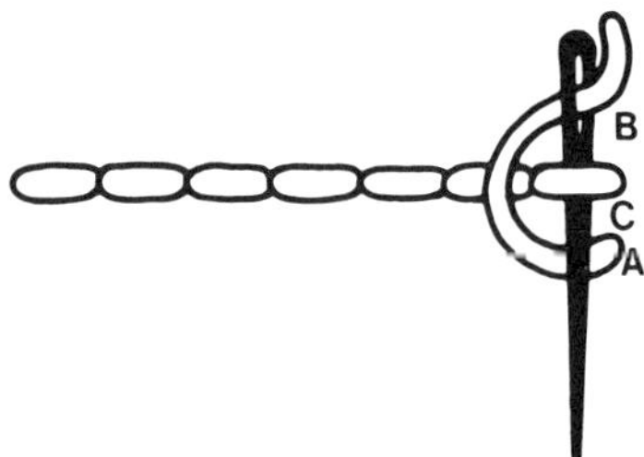

To work this stitch on fabric, first make a border of back stitch, as shown. For needlemade lace, take your stitches right into the braids themselves. This stitch is worked entirely free from the background. Using a blunt needle, come up at A on the right. Go through the first back stitch or braid from B to C. With the thread *under* the needle, just like a buttonhole stitch, draw gently through.

Repeat #1 to the left.

At left is the complete line, going down into the fabric or braid on the last stitch, to secure it.

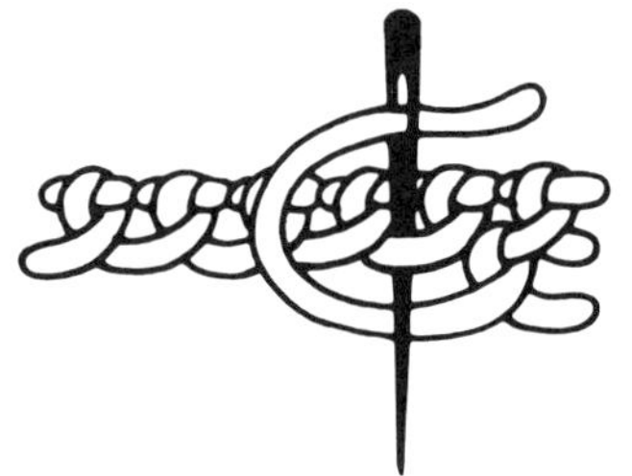

At left is a second row, working again from right to left, and going into each stitch of the previous line, as shown.

For variation, a completely different effect can be formed when you work the first row from right to left, and the second from left to right, as shown here.

Padded appliqué (see page 81).
Designed by Muriel Baker and worked by Mrs. Edward H. Christ

* BURDEN STITCH

This stitch may be used as a filling, or to cover large background spaces. It is attractive worked either very closely so that the basic threads hardly show, or quite wide apart to make an open lacy effect. It has the advantage of being an open filling, yet one where it is very easy to change color. The finished effect is almost like weaving. Generally it is best done in double thread, using the darkest color to underlay it and outlining the finished shape all round afterwards.

Coming up at A, going down at B, up at C, down at D, etc., lay parallel lines about 1/4″ apart (coming up the same side as you go down).

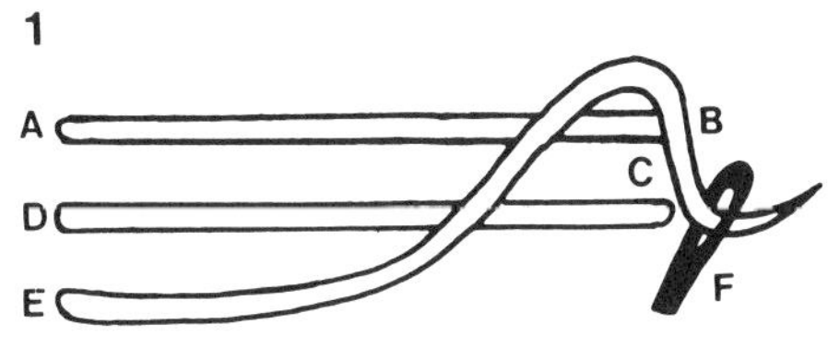

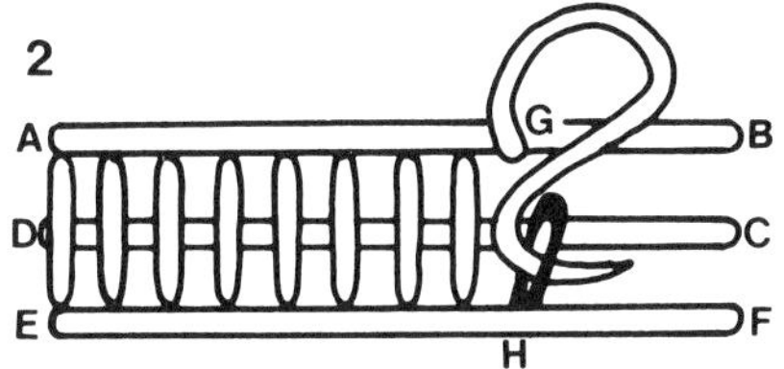

Work the complete line (as shown), coming up at G and going down at H. G is immediately below and *really touching* line A-B; H is immediately above and *really touching* line E-F. Keep all stitches at right angles to the original laid lines.

Coming up at J, just below the line, go down at K, just above the line as in #2. Come up in between the previous stitches, fitting them in like bricks. Again take care to make stitches touch the lines above and below. The finished effect is like weaving, as though the vertical stitches disappear under the horizontal ones.

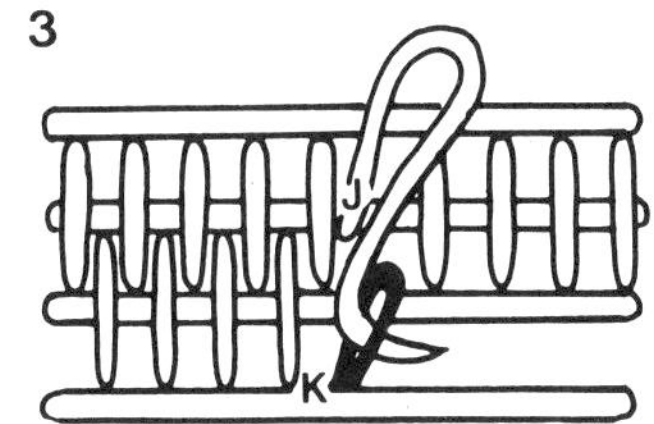

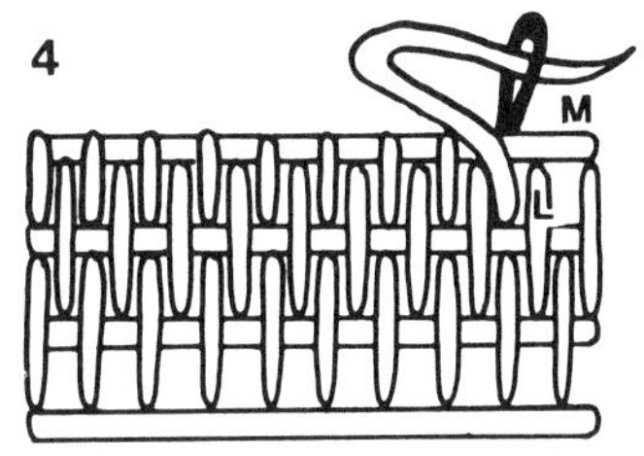

To finish the upper row, come up at L and go down at M, just over the top line. (It is easier to finish the top row of stitching after the scale has been set by the other rows.)

When shading use two needles and completely finish one row before going to the next. In row 3, for instance, work nearly to the center with light color, work one stitch of dark, change to light again, and finish the row. In row 4 work the light stitches, then two stitches of dark, and finish in light. (If all one color were worked first, insufficient space might be left for the other color, causing uneven spacing between stitches.)

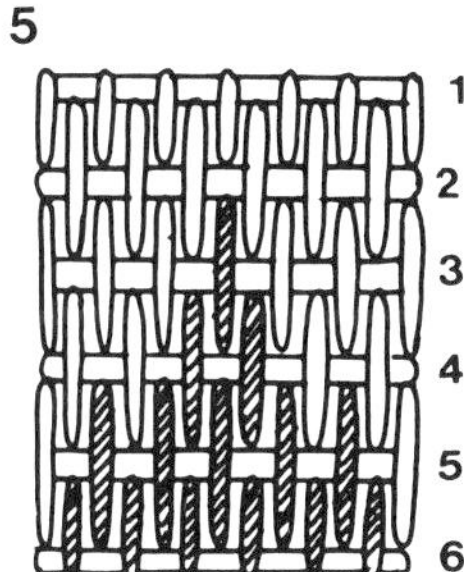

BLOCKING AND MOUNTING

Pressing would be impossible for the raised and embossed embroidery of stump work. Blocking may be difficult if the background fabric is not colorfast, or is made of silk, which could be damaged by water. In this case, the answer is to steam the embroidery. First, mount it on a stretcher frame. Then place an iron upright on the ironing board, set for "linen," and cover it with a wet cloth. Hold the work so that the steam can rise through it from underneath. After five or ten minutes the stitches will stand out clearly, should they have become crushed in working.

If the work is to be framed, raised embroidery should be mounted in a shadow-box frame with plenty of space between the glass and the needlework so that the stitches will not be flattened.